THE LONELIEST RANGER

SELECTED POEMS 1953–2012

Joe Green

MADHAT PRESS
ASHEVILLE, NORTH CAROLINA

MadHat Press
MadHat Incorporated
PO Box 8364, Asheville, NC 28814

Copyright © 2015 Joe Green
All rights reserved

The Library of Congress has assigned
this edition a Control Number of 2015936761

———————

ISBN 978-1-941196-17-5 (paperback)

Text by Joe Green
Cover photograph by Marc Vincenz
Book and cover design by MadHat Press

www.MadHat-Press.com

First Printing

Praise for Joe Green

"I love Joe Green's poetry very much, because it makes me laugh, and because it is sad, and because he is a master of its form and its forms." —**Silke-Maria Weineck, Chair of the Department of Comparative Literature, University of Michigan**

"I have known the poetry of Joe Green for more than a decade, since the early days of *Fulcrum*. And I say, with the fiercest of convictions, that Joe Green is not only one of the tiniest number of poets in our time who are authentic and really matter, but that he is one of the very few contemporary poets who have meant the most to me. Humble to a fault in promoting his own work, this long-needed Selected Poems should finally put Joe on the map where he belongs—as a master of craft and invention, a purveyor of tradition and sensibility and right wonder, an influence upon countless younger poets, and one of our own very few real contemporary classics. May this book flourish widely among poetry lovers everywhere. It is certainly high time." —**Ben Mazer**

"Is there a single contemporary poet who can match Joe Green for comic invention? His poems have more in common with the wide-ranging madness of Voltaire's *Candide* or Nathanael West's *Miss Lonelyhearts* than anything on your poetry shelves. And like those masterpieces of dark comedy, Green's poems have a core that is humane and generous, reading him as restorative as spending time in the sun." —**John Hennessy (author of two collections, *Coney Island Pilgrims* (2013, Ashland Poetry Press) and *Bridge and Tunnel* (2007, Turning Point Books). He teaches at the University of Massachusetts and serves as poetry editor for *The Common*.)**

"Joe Green's poems have lit up journals such as *Fulcrum* for many years, with their surprising turns—alternately allusive, absurd, and personally moving—but always the poems you turn to first because of the pleasure they deliver."   —**David Latane (Professor of English, Virginia Commonwealth University)**

I dreamed I saw Joe Green last night

Alive as he could be

That's not just any Selected Poems

It's THE Sixties Anthology

Here are the lyrical ballads from the Apocalypse we call the Sixties

A definitive mythology of the Sixties

And then some ...   —**Mark Schoor (Executive Director of the Robert Frost Foundation)**

Dedication

To Connie, Johanna and Kris
and to Tim Smith: co-creator and eternal friend.

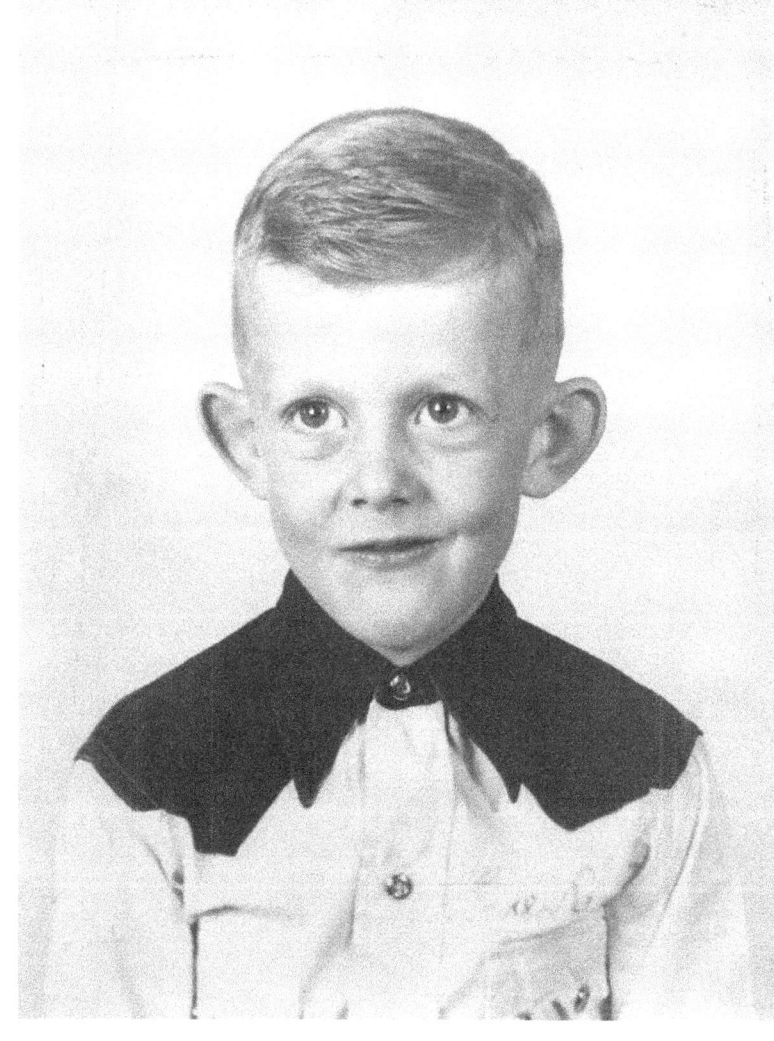

JOE GREEN
THE LONELIEST RANGER
SELECTED POEMS 1953–2012

On Joe Green and His Poetry

Joe Green is a renaissance figure in that today Poetry finds its renaissance in him. I would call him the modern-day Shakespeare if it were not so cliché. A renaissance figure is one who, having internalized our entire poetic tradition—from its origins down to the last minute—to the point of knowing many of its masterpieces by heart, becomes, not the mechanism, but the organism, of its utterly new synthesis: a kind of rebirth. The point is not to "make it new" out of cheap nothing and sheer self-aggrandizement, but to bear it afresh, in the pangs and throes of sacrifice and inspiration. "Making it new" is easy; it is a means for nonpoets and undergraduates to feel good about themselves. On the other hand, giving birth to an all-round poetic synthesis is nearly impossible. Dedicating one's life to this task (that one did not really choose for oneself, that imposes itself uninvited upon the poet) is for the poet merely the first step, the rest being sheer genius, resourcefulness and perseverance.

Curiously, Joe is also the most self-effacing poet I have ever known. We first "met" electronically in the pre-Internet early '90s. There was a poetry group on what was then called Usenet (now archived in Google Groups) where Joe and I were posting poems and blowing off steam. In the later '90s we met face to face and have done so a number of times since. Joe is a poet from head to toe. He has always lived for poetry. Yes in his entire life he never submitted a poem to a magazine uninvited. He was a master poet by the time I first "discovered" him in *Fulcrum* #2 (2003), his first literary publication. We have championed representative selections of Joe's poetry in every subsequent issue of the anthology. However, his work has appeared in very few other publications. (Editors, if you want Joe's writing, you have to ask for it; it's the only way.) He has also self-published a few volumes of hilarious verse, some of which may still be found. I have asked Joe several times why he has not been more active about seeing his writing into print, and he just goes, "I dunno." I suspect it's fatalism, the inner daimon that the poet trusts: a path only for the most daring, the most desperate.

One ironic outcome of his attitude is that this, Joe Green's first real collection of poetry, is his *Selected Poems*, the fruit and distillation of a wild lifetime. It is not what it will seem at first blush. This volume's explosive power is tremendous and self-recharging: I am looking forward to finding out exactly how the blasts, plural, will impact where our poetry goes from here.

Green's verse corpus—his system—is like none other. Historically, very few poets can lay claim to genuine, sui generis uniqueness. His individual poems may—will, are bound to—remind you of various others, but not the whole: the synthesis is all his own. The individual poems work differently and must be understood according to different principles, on a case by case basis. But the whole melds subject and object: the poetry is both the tunnel and the traffic within it.

Trusting its several senses, poetry seeks out the shortest path from heart to heart, leading through a synesthesia of sound, vision, scent, taste, touch, and imagination. Only when intertwined correctly do these work well together to elicit and sustain a focused response in another. The tones may be soft: the tunnel has got fine acoustics. The colors may be subdued: our eyes well-adjusted to the tunnel's lighting. Similarly, the other senses must be well equipped to deal with the traffic conditions inside the tunnel. Scent and touch must not distract, but correspond. All these sensory proportions are balanced perfectly in Green. The threads of poetic conversation that pull you along your path are strong yet gentle, never domineering. He does not unleash a chaos upon you. Instead, the poet speaks to you as his equal, a fellow dweller in the same spacetime and manifold of the senses.

Philosophically speaking, the human being is built in some correspondence with the world, is adequate to it. Our senses must be well attuned to be able to cope with what is within and without us. However, we first "disordered" them at Rimbaud's behest (we should have stopped at a similar age!), and now we find ourselves living in wiseass, speculative times where dry-as-dust "discourse" has invaded our poetry wholesale. It is dead on arrival: the intellectual has lost the interlocutor, the interlocutor has lost interest. By contrast, Joe Green parachutes us plumb out of the soporific stratosphere of idle propositions and back onto the rivers and oceans and dry land of our earth. He never lets go of the thread of conversation, of camaraderie, a reassurance of sanity. In his lyric poems he is speaking specifically to you, up close and personal, in the intimate words that he and you have in common.

Joe Green's verse is merry against all odds, in the face of all tragedy (there is something Irish or Russian about that, though Joe is only half Irish). His tragicomedy is full of suspense, dialogic, polyphonic, masterful, and fantastically real. The poet tells it like it is, and keeps his promises. He has promised us "a diamond at the end of time," and he delivers. I've already got mine, now you go get it!

—*Philip Nikolayev*

CONTENTS

On Joe Green and His Poetry – Philip Nikolayev	ix
Sonnet: The Sense of an Ending	1
In 1953	2
Bell, Book and Candle	3
A Lone Ranger Christmas	5
I Think Continually Of Those Who Are Truly Late	8
My father in the store commanding "Buy!"	10
Oh, Donna	11
The Snow	14
The Iliad of Joe Green	16
Argentinean Black Catholic Jew	21
How My Mother Gave Up Drinking Gin	25
A Christmas Story	28
I Remember a Halloween of Long Ago	30
I Had a Friend Named Johnny Wasko	32
The Ballad of Steve	34
I Look Out and I Hear the Knell	39
Another Christmas Poem	41
The Ballad of Ernie White	43
Twilight Zone	44
Jipijapa Hat	46
The Diamond at the End of Time	47
The Ballade of Susie Lamont	57
1968	58

Go Tell the Achyans	59
Kevin Anent Jimi	61
I Love Them Old Hippies	63
A Ballade	64
The Ballad of Little Noddy	73
Jim Moore	91
Ara Killijian	93
Fort Dix	94
Where Are You Now Charlie Solomon?	95
Oh, My	99
Once There Was Childermas Gazelles	104
The Ballad of Miss Victoria Minh	105
Ronald Reagan Blues	108
Luftmensch	109
Point Lobos: 1944	110
The Insect Clerks of Neiman Marcus	114
A Short History	117
At the Hospital	121
Dinosaur Love	122
Old Father	123
Halloween	125
Just Spring with Chaucer and Some Shriners	128
In the Blue Note	130
Chiasmus in Chicago	131
Trio	133
Alienation Effect	135

The Loneliest Ranger: Selected Poems

My Left Foot	136
The Rain	137
Ok, then … so we're in Fredonia …	138
The Grasshopper and the Ant	139
The Red Light Is The Blue Light Is	142
Incident on Fifty-second Street	144
Coatesville 1	145
Coatesville 2	
Last Night	146
A Very Fine Fiddle Had She	148
My Demented Mother	149
After Twitter	150
Old Poet Yellowknife	152
What is Poetry?	155
Trout Fishin' in Yellowknife	157
A Catholic Negro in Pittsburgh	159
The Tale of the Tinker Transported	161
Kwanzaa Christmas Tango	165
Night of the Hunter	167
That	170
My Mojo All Gone	171
The Cats of Paree	172
Ship Poem	174
Christopher Smart	175
Tiny Tim Blues	177
You Are a Star	178

Arrayed for the Bridal	179
No More A-Roving	181
Dreamland	182
Some Last Words	183
Canarios or The Escape of D.B. Cooper	184
Vaudeville	186
Third Murderer	187
Poem Written at Twenty Below	189
The Tall Hair Blues	191
To Tim Smith	193
Timothy L. Smith	194
Outta Here	195
The Stars The Stars	
All the Holy Night	196
Something to Count On	
The Plum Wine of the Buddha	
In Martini Veritas	197
Night, Fog, War	
Introduction to the Rin Tin Tin Poems	198
Late for a Poetry Reading	200
Los Marielitos	203
The Defiant Ones	205
No, I Am Not Prince Hamlet Nor Was Meant To Be	208
New York City—Toward Night	210
In Loneliest Country	211
1953	213

L.A. Song	215
Breakfast at Tiffany's	216
What a Little Moonlight Can Do	218
After the First Death, Well …	221
Road Kill	222
The Thing	223
RinTinTology	224
The Platinum Goddess	226
Boulez, Bloch, Maurice Ravel	228
Letter from a Dog Before Troy	229
All the Starry Animals	230
Old Dog: A Villanelle	231
I Died In New York	232
My Epitaph	235
Jazz Life/Afterlife	236
Before Another Poetry Reading	238
Epigraph	240

From the Limerick Odyssey

Book Twelve: The Sirens, Scylla and Charybdis, the Cattle of the Sun	241
Books Thirteen through Twenty-Four	249
Orson Welles interviews Joe Green	254
Acknowledgements	271
About the Author	273

Sonnet: The Sense of an Ending

In Faerie Tales if the ant king says to kill your horse
Then you better do it, especially if you want the girl and the gold
And all the coupons. Standing by the waterfall you think
That everything has changed and you are not sure why

And then the Czar comes riding along and next thing you know
You are at the ball with your ratskin gloves and your sneer
And the chance to die defeating Napoleon and a sleigh
Will whiz you away that night and you dance—
the moon, the Neva then—

The great train to Moscow. And then who should leap
Beneath the train? Anna! Anna! And you say something in French
And the train moves on as do the stars whirling
So that—at the end—you end up in Paris

And, on the boulevard you walk you walk
And, one night, pass the young Baudelaire. Tip your hat.
You are dying, dying.

Joe Green

In 1953

In 1953
I was in our living room
Reading the comics.
"Dondi," I think.
And the headline in the part of the paper I
Put aside said:

"STALIN DEAD!"

And my father came home from work
And took off his hat
And I asked him
"Who was Stalin, Dad?"
And he said

"He was a bad man, son."
And reached in his pocket
And flipped me a silver dollar!

Now let's all watch
As that silver dollar

falls.

Bell, Book and Candle

I always liked Kim Novak
In *Bell, Book and Candle*
Curled up on that couch
Which you would describe as
Immensely red, but you are wrong
For the colors that show best by candlelight
Are (she tells you) white, carnation and
And a kind of sea-water green
And Pyewacket, that lucky cat
Curled up next to you, green eyes
And a sardonic glance
And you reach for the silver cigarette lighter
Man, you are as shaky as Jimmy Stewart
And it is Christmas! Christmas!
And you know she is a witch and
You want to ask her
Why she, well … has a tree.… Let the room
Abound in light especially
Colored and varied
Or something like that. Witch? Christmas?
And she gets up and is on
Tiptoes placing the ornament just so
("oes and spangs as they are of no great cost")
On the tree and she knows what you are
Looking at. She knows.

Christmas? But if you ask she'll say
Something like "The best art is general"
Which, really, you haven't heard before
And she turns and the doors to the balcony

Joe Green

Open and snow swirls you out and you
Are both on the balcony. Manhattan!
And you know that Gene Kelly is
There somewhere feeling just a bit blue
But will anyway dance his way into
Someone's heart tonight and snow is
Steepling on the Chrysler Building and
There is giant impossible yellow moon
And she is there and you

Know this poem ain't going to end the way
You want it to.

A Lone Ranger Christmas

My personal space is being renovated
And Christmas is coming.
That beige suede couch had to go
And it will be a week before
Miss Alexa Hampton Papageorgiou
Stepdaughter to Count Mario Loreta Frusci di Bertinoro
(that horrible man) and Nathalie Farman-Farma
Will along with other
Young Friends to Save Venice
Arrive with my 18th-Century Venetian
Toiletry case so how will everything be
Ready for the Mr. Jimmy Stewarts who
Every Christmas bringing along Mr. Danny Kaye
Who is a bore but is after all
Mr. Danny Kaye? They expect tea and my conversation
(I never mention *It's A Wonderful Life*)
On Christmas Eve and how will I then
In all good conscience the Mr. Jimmy Stewarts
And Mr. Danny Kaye being as it were homeless
On the eve of the birth of the Christ Child
Proceed as is my wont to Harlem
Where a bevy of jazz combos
Of the good old sort play
Alluringly shining in the candlelit mirrors
As I sip brandy and recover
All lostnessesess.

There is a certain slant of snow
I can see from my analyst's office

That promises that someone very like
Theda Bara will soon come into my life.

But stepping, as it were, BACK into
Cinderella's coach, past midnight and
5 o'clock in the afternoon
in Coatesville I find fuck it
I am as it were (I wish) back in Coatesville.
Flush then out into the PA slush a man
In uniform with a job to do leaving merrily
The St. Regis a very nice hotel bar of *The Shining*
Sort and at least I ain't at the Bongo yet
Like my friend John sitting there all his
One-dollar bills on the bar showing he has
A right to stay. No, I ain't doing so well
But at least I have a job and going down 2nd Ave.
Past the coal yard Christ does any other town
Still have a coal yard past the Polack kids
Sitting on their Flexible Flyers smoking Pall Malls
Past Giancola's Barbers where for thirty years
He has had up a 1963 calendar showing a kid
Getting run over by someone very like
Hugh Beaumont who is horrified that his '59
Buick hit this kid and he is drunk Don't
Drive Drunk past Trionfetti's bar same neon Martini
Glass winking green in the window. I'll bet my
Grandmother wished she were still alive so
She could walk by me wishing she could just
Walk on by me never looking at me at all
Her loser grandson so I stop in Trionfetti's
For a little drink. 41 and back in town.

I'll be late for work. This must be the
Very last JC Penneys and here I am my
Man Just give me the motherfucking bell.

—*The Loneliest Ranger*

Joe Green

I Think Continually Of Those Who Are Truly Late.

I think continually of those who are truly late.
Like old John Howe in the snow
Leaning against my father's store.
"Open Christmas eve! Open until eight!"
Which it was about an hour before.
John's drunk. Pulls hard on the oarlocks.
Stagolees across the street to the Polacks.
"Just one drink," Stan says. "Then you gotta go."
John don't say nothing.' Waves his hand.
 Means "I know."

At our house the night is anything but holy and calm.
John's there. "Jimmie, I need a present
For my boy Tom."
Just like last year. I sense disaster.
I'm right. "Here it is, John. Already wrapped.
A Talkin' Viewmaster. "
John says "I gotta go." My dad says "Let's go outside.
I'll take you home. Looks like you could use a ride."
My mother says "Dammit, all you kids
Need to get to bed."
My uncle says "It's been what?
Fifteen years since his boy's been dead?"

The Christmas star rages. With what? With glory?
I don't know. Anyway, this is a true Christmas story.

I think continually of those who are truly late.
And how they also serve
Who can barely stand ... but wait.

Joe Green

My father in the store commanding "Buy!"

My father in the store commanding "Buy!"
And they did. My dad knew why.
Went in for a lamp and out they went:
With a bedroom soot—store credit at six percent
And a plaster matador thrown in to put before
On the porch near the sofa near the row house door.
But me? I was indifferent—indifferent very
Downtown I went to the movies and then the library.
Library closing I glided past the Coatesville Hotel
Dreaming of men with atomic brains. I wasn't doing so well.
Across the street saw my dad with all those World War
        Depression men.
Smoking Chesterfields and Luckies. Chewing Sen Sen.
Almost all gone. Almost all now just dust and ash and bone.
And I hurried home to watch *The Twilight Zone*.

OH, DONNA

On one Christmas Eve I was staying up late.
Reading and reading. Ah, nineteen fifty-eight!
Under the covers. By a Scout flashlight's beam.
The immortal poesy of a Midsummer Night's dream.
But I knew I was in trouble. The reason's because
I kinda liked Jesus but I loved Santa Claus.
Ah, I remember as through a black mist
That Jesus was very far down on my list:
I loved *Famous Monsters*, my Davy Crockett lampshades,
Sugar Ray Robinson and Gillette Blue Blades.
I liked Classic Comics and wasn't too fancy:
Loved Mutt and Jeff but couldn't stand "Nancy."
I hated Johnny De Matteo. But I loved his bike.
Liked to sleep on the patio and I didn't like Ike.
Loved *Highway Patrol* and really loved *Topper*.
If he'd been around I would have liked Dennis Hopper.
I'd read the *Iliad* and liked that madman Achilles
Loved Chico Fernandez—shortstop for the Phillies.
Liked watching my neighbor Maria Cantonese
Run screaming from me with my jarful of bees.
Liked the Lone Ranger and, of course, Rin Tin Tin.
Liked that old movie about Gunga Din.
I knew I was screwed up. Knew I was wrong.
But Jesus was nothing compared to King Kong.
But I knew I was in trouble. The reason's because
I kinda liked Jesus but I loved Santa Claus.
But that Christmas Eve I was reading the Bard.
Went to bed early. It always was hard
Waiting for all of those hours to pass.
Until my mom and dad came back from Mass.

Santa wouldn't arrive until they went to bed.
"I heard there's a storm" my uncle Joe said.
"He'll probably make it but I thought you'd like to know
That he's stuck in a blizzard up near Buffalo."
So I went up to bed and he said "Good luck!"
And I stayed awake reading about Bottom and Puck.
Then turned off the flashlight. My thoughts were so far
From our savior Jesus and the Christmas star.
Then ... what was that sound? I turned on my pillow.
Looked out the window. It was Donna Fruillo.
Undressing! She must have forgotten to put down the shade!
Donna Fruillo! She was in the tenth grade.
The light went off in a flash but I saw what I saw.
Donna was naked! Was naked! And all
Thoughts of Christmas, of Santa, the Bard!
Disappeared in an instant. Something was ... hard.
This was so strange! And then my little hand
Crept under the covers as an angel band
Wept and cried out! But, what did I know?
I said to myself. "This is what Heaven's like, Joe.
Grace directly from Jesus!" I finished and then
Prayed to Lord Jesus for it to happen again.
What a discovery! And that Christmas day
I found many fine reasons to lie down and pray
Up in my bedroom behind my locked door.
If I had known about this ... I would have loved Jesus before!
Again and again I was open to Heaven.
Again and again. My record was seven
Times in one night. I just offered a prayer
And thought of Oh Donna and Jesus was there.
But then all was ruined. On that New Year's Eve
I told Johnny Doan how I'd come to believe.

How Jesus saved me. How my soul he did win.
And Johnny said gravely "That's a mortal sin.
Right now you are headed directly to Hell."
And I looked right at him and told him "Oh, well.
I guess I can go to hell if I wanna."
And I cried out nightly "Oh, Donna! Oh, Donna!"

Joe Green

The Snow

Because you loved the old man
You tell stories about him.
Sometimes the stories are true.

He spit tobacco in tin cans and lived
In your aunt's house in an upstairs room
Where she was not allowed.

He pissed out the window when
He was drunk and sang
"Arthur McBride."

Your aunt screamed,
"Sweet Jesus, what's this?"
And he looked down on her.

"It's your goddamned father
Pissing out the goddamned window!"

The winter night when
He died you were home looking
Out at the snow.

At the loneliness of the footprints
Your parents had made
Where they had gone.

At yours where you had gone out
And then come in again.

Small flakes floated past the streetlamps
And melted when they touched
The car. The wavering lights

Shivered, standing in pools of themselves.

When you parents came home
The snow had already whitened
Their shoulders and he was dead.

The next morning when you awoke,
The new snow had come.

And your father's footprints
And your mother's and
Yours and everyone's were all gone.

But the new world was still
So lovely all in the new snow.

Joe Green

The Iliad of Joe Green

I beat up the Gamashay twins.
It was back in '63.
My friend Johnny said to me
"Do you know what you've done?
Do you know what you've done, Joe?
Do you know what you've done?"

I looked up to my friend John.
Looked up from my book.
My book was the Iliad.
I gave a John a dirty look.
"There's no balm in Gilead
For those moronic twins.
I caught the bastards going out.
And caught them going in.

It was my left hook, John.
It was my left hook."

"Did you forget their cousin Frank?"
Johnny said to me.
"He's built just like an M1 tank
And he's back in town you see.
He's 16 and he's damn insane.
He already has a beard.
He'll take you like a freight train.
Plus he's really weird."

I looked at John. Put down my book.
I'm sure my eyes did narrow.
Then I gave John a frightened look.
Thought of the falling of the sparrow.
"Tell me John, say it ain't true.
Their cousin from Wilkes-Barre?
Their cousin from Wilkes-Barre?"

"Yes, that's who I mean, Joe.
Yes, that's who I mean."

I ran back into my room.
Stayed there for a week.
I read and read the Iliad
But I was somewhat meek.
I tried to think just what to do
And concluded I would run.
Living in Honolu -lu -lu
Might be rather fun.

But the best and well laid lams
Often go astray.
My mother she did come to me
At the dawning of the day.
"It's a perfectly nice day outside.
I want you to go out.
I'm taking your library card.
Go ahead and pout.

Go ahead and pout Joe, go ahead and pout."

I knew then my doom had come.
So I snuck out outside.
"Look here the bastard is!"
The Gamashay twins cried!
And there like some damn dinosaur
Stood their cousin Frank.
He was taller that he was before.
Still built like an M1 tank. Lord!
Still built like an M1 tank.

"Come here, you little shithouse rat"
Cousin Frank did cry.
And I saw just where my doom was at
And knew that I would die.
But then I thought "If all is lost
To Hell with all these willies.
I would pay a terrible cost.
But I'd take it like Achilles."

And so I sneered at Cousin Frank
And started spouting Greek:
The first lines of the Iliad.
I prayed my soul to keep.
I almost got up to that part,
The great part in Line 9
When I heard Line 10
In Homeric Greek
And the voice it wasn't mine.

The voice it wasn't mine!

I stopped and stood in wonder
Seeing what I saw.
There was a clap of thunder.
Oh, the Gods exclaimed in awe.
It was Cousin Frank reciting
Homer's immortal verse.
He was weak on the pluperfect.
But, by God, I had heard worse.

Weak on the pluperfect.
But, by God, I had heard worse.

And Frank and I smiled one to one
And left the rest behind.
Two youths in a steel mill town
Loving the life of the mind.

We fell into discussion
Of Homer's metaphors
And just what Herodotus said
Of all those damn Greek wars.

Frank and I strode out right then
From that steel mill town.
I mean this metaphorically.
You better write it down.
I went on to a wild, wild youth.
Frank stayed on the straight and narrow.
And in three years led the Classics Club
At the University of Wilkes-Barre.

Joe Green

So come all of ye strange young lads
Who love the classics well
But despair of ever leaving
The awful steel mill hell.
Pay heed to this fine story
And know you might be free:
Leaving the steel mills behind
For the wine-dark sea!

Argentinean Black Catholic Jew

I. Cante

He was an Argentinean Black Catholic Jew
It's too bad but I am one too.
How sadly I think of my father!

After Mass he would play
"Hernando's Hideaway"
Then the Blues, then yell at my mother.

After Mass he would play
"Hernando's Hideaway"
And bitch of the Schwartzes and Yentels.

Then damn the Ofays
And, in his own special way,
Evict some of the Yids from his rentals.

II. Cante Cante

Take a Jew. Take my father.

Born in the beginning of the 20th century—
that century of universal disaster.

Born in the USA to a family of neurotic vaudevillians:

African American Jews who disguised their Jewishness
and pretended to be an Argentinian family of tango dancers.

Joe Green

An African American Jew dancing the tango:
the one dance that, above all, speaks of fatality,
of destinies engulfed in pain. It is the dance of sorrow.

Then take this Jew (my poor Papa)
and arrange it so that he falls in love in Berlin
months before Hitler takes over ...

Falls in love with that fatal woman: Ilsa.

The rest of the family flees while my Papa—the fake gaucho—is drawn inexorably into the darkest of the dark underworlds that existed in Berlin: the Nosferatu: the secret society of decadents with their Vampire balls and Grand Guignol orgies

and my father and Ilsa dancing *El tango de la muerte* there while Europe descended into madness and my father danced—

danced to the dark music of the bandoneon and the violin:

A long stillness as the watchers waited in the dark and my father and Ilsa waited frozen on the stage and then

the quick motion that begins the tango!

stillness ...

and then the sudden violence—

the dynamic of a frozen world suddenly shattered,

the apotheosis of the twentieth century!

III. Cante Cante Cante

I stepped out into the night from the funeral home remembering
how horrible it must have been for my father
to pretend he was a Catholic.

This explained his strange melancholy
during my first holy communion and,
as I remembered more of the story he told me,
I thought back to those times when,
my mother gone to Novena,
how he would lock himself into the bedroom
and all we could would hear was "Hernando's Hideaway"
on the old record player and

the sounds of my father shuffling about,

breathing …

IV. Cante Cante Cante Cante

Ilsa said "I am IRA.
And I think I can get us away.
But you must be baptized
And then in disguise
We'll go to the U S of A!"

They fled cross the dark Irish sea.
My mother was Ilsa you see
And they remained in good health
And Pope Pius the Twelfth

Joe Green

Cried fie and fiddle dee dee!
Then they came to these shores at last
But the fad for the tango had passed
What could a Jew do?
So he did a soft shoe
Grateful that he wasn't gassed.
He starred in some old minstrel show
Papa said he wanted to go
Mama said "You Black Jew
You're working for two.

Dance—it's all that you know."

How My Mother Gave Up Drinking Gin

Christmas eve of fifty-seven my mother gave up drinking gin.
She kicked me out into the snow and wouldn't let me in.
"Freeze your pagan keister Mister Joseph Green
You can stay outside till Easter making fun of Bishop Sheen!"

She was drinking Christmas cocktails with my uncle Joe
Who had drunk up all the whiskey. He denied it but I know.
They had run flat out of vermouth and you know just what that
    yields:
The telling of the Awful Truth while smoking Chesterfields.

Uncle Joe confessed to Mama and told her he was gay.
My Mama said "Oh, no you're not and what an Awful Thing to
    say."
I was watching TV and said "Look there, Uncle Joe!
He acts just like you do sometimes!" Joe just said "I know."

I pounded on the door and wept "Oh, mama I will freeze!"
Then slipped and fell on the front porch steps and fell down to
    my knees.
I raved and begged and then I prayed. Then gave a little shout.
When a gentle voice behind me said "Now, what's this all about?"

And I heard celestial music and peered into the night.
Oh, it was the Virgin Mary all dressed in blue and white!
Yes, it was the Virgin Mary! Ask me how I know.
She looked like a Maid of Derry but had a snake beneath her toe!

And there inside a pink cloud was a merry angel choir
And kind of to the left were all the martyrs in a fire
And then there were the patriarchs and little Johnny Doan
Who was baptized by my Mama when they left him all alone.

Whose parents thought he died last year a Baptist to the last
But was re-baptized by my Mama and so went to heaven fast
With all the other Catholics. She saved him from the Hell
Of the awful Baptist heaven. He was happy, I could tell!

For there was St. John Bosco and St. Sebastian too!
But Johnny didn't answer when I shouted "How are you?
I'm freezing here. Help me out!" But I couldn't see him through
    the swarm
Of Catholic saints all wanting to … just keep him safe and
    warm.

"Oh help me Blessed Mother. There's no room at the Inn
For my mother and my uncle Joe are inside drinking gin!"
But … yes it was St Patrick! And he said "No, lad she ain't
I know your uncle Joe's a homo but your mother is a saint!"

Saint Pat raised up his crozier and cried "Erin go Bragh!"
And Mama was so embarrassed as instantly she saw
All the saints and angels and the Blessed Mother too
Float into our living room. What else could she do?

"O, Lord I am not worthy! Oh, help me in my sin!
For it's the eve of Christmas and I sit here drinking gin
For Joe drank up the whiskey and I fear there's none around
And I have no drink to give you." There was hardly any sound

Till the Blessed Virgin Mary said with her charming Irish lilt:
"Ah, there's no need to worry. I absolve you of your guilt.
For we have good Irish whiskey—the finest you have seen.
Ego te absolvo! Where's the glasses Mrs. Green?

And turn off that damn homo. We'll have no more of sin.
Turn on Perry Como and let the Sacred in!

Just turn on Perry Como and let the Sacred in!"

Uncle Joe was quite offended at that awful "homo" slur
But, of course, he just pretended for he knew just who they were.
And he joined the Host of Heaven as they danced a jig aerobic.
They were Irish and were Catholic and so, of course, quite
        homophobic!

Then suddenly all rested and beamed with angel joy
As good old Perry Como sang "The Little Drummer Boy."
"Thank God for the Irish," the Blessed Mother said
And I crept up into my room to read James Joyce: *The Dead*.

And put my special music on and watched the general snow
And wondered what was going on and danced a slow tango.

Joe Green

A Christmas Story

When I was real little
My dad would tuck me into bed.
"You get to sleep. You know Mr. Jackson is watching."
Mr. Jackson was our chief of police
Scrawny and sixty.
And I imagined him leaning a ladder
Up against my window and shining
His flashlight in to check to see
If I was asleep. "Night," my dad would say
And, as I remember it, pausing in
The dark hall way to light a cigarette Bogie style
And then his footsteps going away.
And then no more.
Later I remember going upstairs to bed
By myself. I put the light on
And read *Famous Monsters*: a fan
Magazine for those who loved them all:
Frankenstein, Werewolf, Dracula.
And I believed I was right.
Dracula would kick all their asses.
But when I got the book from the library
I didn't even make it to the village inn.
Too damn scared and even scared
With the book under my bed.

Yes, it was strange in the Fifties.
Mr. Frank Stefanik who worked in the mill
And lived behind us with his dog Oscar
Saw a flying saucer and it was in the papers.
A week late he fell off a crane. Dead.

Mars is calling. We all were waiting.

At school I had a friend Steve
Who they called "Sputnik"
Since he was as smart and as wearied as Bob Dylan at sixty
When he was seven. And you could listen
To the real sputnik beeping on his stepfather's
Shortwave and we deserved Rod Serling

Yes, he was inevitable. We had all of that
Under Cheyenne Mountain. Waiting.

Steve would come to school
With a big black eye and tell everyone
How he got beat up by black shapes
But we knew it was his stepfather.

And twenty years later I met him
In a bar and he told me
How he was just driving across a bridge
After his divorce coming back
From visiting his kids and pulled over
And just jumped in the river but
Then changed his mind …
And he laughed and we talked
About *Famous Monsters*. He still held out
For the Werewolf but there was
Something else and he did kill himself
Before the year was out.
And I'll always remember how we
Both leaned on the bar after he told his story.
Waiting for something worse to happen.

Joe Green

I Remember a Halloween of Long Ago

I remember a Halloween of long ago.
There was a Halloween moon.
I was going to go with my uncle Joe.
"When will he be here?" "Soon."

I sat and waited by the front porch light
And watched as the ghouls crept by.
The leaves tumbled down in the Halloween night.
The clouds were orange in the sky.

With moonlight shining on the steel mill red
As the old and familiar hell.
And Uncle Joe was beside me.... Said
"You're ready, I guess? Oh, well."

And we began walking the dreary beat
I walked every Hallow's eve
To the houses there on our sad street
Just where I wanted to leave.

When my uncle said, "C'mon, get in"
As we came up to his car.
Ah, he had a flask and it was full of gin
And the car was a Jaguar.

Silver and white like a god's own ghost
And Joe put it in first gear
Then second and third and then began to coast
And sing like a gondolier.

And I could feel the moon laugh down at us
As we glided through the night.
"Let's just drive," my uncle said.
And I just said, "All right!"

Joe Green

I Had a Friend Named Johnny Wasko

I had a friend named Johnny Wasko.
He died on Halloween.
Had a friend named Johnny Wasko.
Died on Halloween.

"And he was a good boy," the old nun said.
"Not like you, Mr. Joseph Green."

Mr. Joseph Green.

Next year Halloween wind blowing
There was a big full moon.
That Halloween wind was blowing.
Big old yellow full moon.
Took my Halloween candy.
Gonna put it on Johnny's tomb.

Walk through Fairview Cemetery
Up to Johnny's grave.
Walk through Fairview Cemetery
Up to Johnny's grave.
Gonna give him all my candy.
My poor soul to save.

Gave him one Sugar Daddy.
I don't like them anyway.
He always liked Sugar Daddys
When he came out to play.
Put down the Sugar Daddy.
Then I walked away.

Little skeleton six feet under.
Little skeleton walking away.
Little skeleton six feet under.
Little skeleton walking away.
Lit a Salem cigarette and kept walking.
Had nothing else to say.

Joe Green

The Ballad of Steve

After all of these years it's hard to believe
That I never wrote a ballad for my old friend Steve
Who jumped off a bridge in Boston one day
And called a bit later, said "I just have to say
I jumped off a bridge and found out I'm gay!
And I'm calling you now just to report
I'll be on a jet plane from Logan Airport.
I'm leaving now. I just gotta go.
On a jet plane to San Francisco.
Remember me now like you remember me then
For I won't go back to the straight life again!"

We were in the first grade and Sister Edwin Marie
Said "I want you two hoodlums to come out here with me."
We went out to the hallway and she turned and hissed
"You better know, you bold articles, that you're on my list."
Then she pulled out a copybook that we had left on the bus.
With art on its pages that was signed by us.
"I don't care that you mock me but, boys, at the least
You shouldn't be mocking God's holy priest."
Steve had drawn Father Keegan. I had drawn Donald Duck.
Sticking a pitchfork in his fat ass. Good luck!
Good luck to you boys. You're headed to Hell.
Well, that was implied and we both thought "Oh, well."

Now, poor Steve's father was happy and smart.
A nice guy, a great dad but he had a bad heart.
But in spite of it all Steve had some hope:
His dad was doing better and had a great telescope.
And he took Steve out on a clear Saturday night

To a far field near Honey Brook away from the lights
Of the steel mill, et cetera, that made up Coatesville
And put his hand on his shoulder as they stood on a hill
To point out the planets. And there he dropped dead.
"I loved my dad." was all that Steve said
Many years later as we sat in some bar
After Steve had said "No" to the Vietnam war.

Should I continue? Steve might say "Why bother?"
But by the fifth grade Steve had an asshole stepfather
Who would beat him and tell him: "You make me sick.
You think you're so smart you little Sputnik.
Let's see how good you are ... you dumb little joker.
Sit down right now and play me in poker."
At least that's what Steve told me ... but what he told me still
    sings!
"He had four Jacks. But I had four Kings!"
I never believed him but let the story abide.
And in the fifth grade Steve tried suicide.
Ran into the woods with twenty feet of old rope.
Now, I hope you believe me. It's good to hope.
Steve ran through the woods then fell down on his back
And tied his sad ass to a railroad track.
He had dug through gravel right under a tie.
Steve said, "I was serious. I wanted to die."
And he stayed there all night. "The thing was in the main—
I waited and waited for that goddamn train.
I think. I don't know. I might have fallen asleep...."
But here's a last fact that would make the bad angels weep.
His mom ... the next morning ... found a note on his bed.
"I'd told them just where I would be," poor Steve said.
His stepfather found him. Tied up in the rope.

"Trains don't run down this track anymore, you damn dope."
There was no one else there. The man lifted Steve's head.
"Trains don't come down this track anymore," the man said.

Then Steve became bad—a blot and a blister!
God said "That little punk" and sent Sister Eucharista!
She came from a Dago school in South Philly
From whence God had sent her with a view to a kill.
He said, "Sister, you're done with those wops at Don Bosco
Smite that little smart-ass. Smite Steven Wasko!"

She arrived at our school one drear day in December.
How the Earth groaned! Cried "Remember, remember
All that is mortal may be destroyed in an instant.
All living must die. When you think about it isn't it
Fucked? There you go. Dammit. God is the boss of us.
Is it any damn wonder he would send a colossus
To destroy a small boy who could grow up to be gay?"
Yes, that's just what the Earth was saying that day.

She entered our room. I sat like a Quaker.
Then I heard a rough voice, "I think I can take her."
A voice blent with doom. I'll never forget he
Will e'er be remembered—brave Tom Trionfetti!
The toughest kid there and of an obsolete race
And the only fifth-grader with his own parking space.
Flunked how many times? He was almost sixteen
And looked like a cobra but was six times as mean.
His dad owned a bar and brave Tom would go
After school to the bar to hang out with Negroes!
Guys named Spiderhead, Bantu, Bullet and Baby.
And sometimes after school Tom would say "Maybe

Today is the day that I kick your dumb ass."
But if you cringed and you whimpered, he'd give you a pass.
He had places to go! He had no time to stop.
And all fell before him—a brave Negro-Wop.
A scandal to all. To the American nation!
But I cried "Hurrah!" for miscegenation
As I heard his fine words (though spoken quite lowly)
Then the evil nun turned and said distinctly and slowly:
"Why did God make you? Mr. Trionfetti?"
Who replied "I don't know." Now, I'm willing to bet he
Just in that instant felt the meaning of fear
As the nun said, quite weirdly "Just come here, my dear.
Let's look at God's world. Just open the window."
Which he did ah, he did! We all felt an ill wind blow
From heaven into our fifth-grade classroom
As brave Tom smiled nervously awaiting his doom
As the nun smiled like a camp guard at Camp Bergen-Belsen
And seized brave Tom in a quite effective Half-Nelson
Hoisted him up and in an instant the fated
Brave Negro-Wop was defenestrated!

And all the class screamed. Steve cried "Oh, no! Oh, no!"
It looked like the evil nun was letting him go!
But Sister Eucharista held on to poor Tom
Who screamed, the poor boy. Sister Eucharista stayed calm.
Thirty feet down! Well, twenty at least.
But Sister just smiled like an unholy beast.
Then Steve Wasko stood up and cried "Stop it, you bitch!"
Which had an effect on the mad nun—one which
Was ordained, one suspects, in celestial realms
Where contempt for the heathen quite overwhelms
All of the talking points about charity, caritas,

And the fact of defiance leaves one quite at a loss
Except to, of course, smite the goddamned young heathen
Which is what, God knew, was waiting for Steven.
The nun jerked brave Tom in. He collapsed on the floor.
"God won't have to put up with you anymore!"
She seized Steve by the wrist. Dragged Steve to the casement.
Which appalled even the damned down in Hell's basement
Who raised a confused, a "half-human" cheer
For Steve—who smiled calmly, showing no fear
As the nun heaved him outside and he, hanging, suspended
Inspired all the damned in red burial blended
As he cried "Fuck you, bitch. There's one thing I know.
You're a big dumb chickenshit! C'mon, let me go!"

The mad nun hauled him in! She started to cry.
Then fled from the room to the sweet bye and bye.
Never heard from again. Deemed quite insane!
And the next month Steve's stepfather was killed by a crane.
Which quite cheered Steve up. Made him blithe and so bonny.
As he moved through the grades singing "Hey, nonney nonney!"
And always alone. He had become as a God.
Which, of course, drives one crazy and makes one quite odd.
You marry your cousin. Deny "Ecce Homo!"
You are Andy Warhol but prefer Perry Como.
Throw yourself off a bridge. Then change your mind.
And decide that you'll leave the straight life behind!
Head out to Frisco to see what fate brings
Which, for Steve, meant that he would move to Palm Springs
With his only beloved. The guy Kismet sent:
A software engineer with a Limey accent.
And there they live now. But it's hard to believe.
That this is the end of the ballad of Steve.

I Look Out and I Hear the Knell

I look out and I hear the knell
From my room in the Coatesville Hotel.
Oh, why can't it be as it was before
A few years after '54?

In fact it would be great
If we could go back to '58.
And I think it would be my plan
To be kinder to Richie Holleran

Who has been buried since—I quite forget.
No matter. I can see him yet.
At the age of ten in Central Park
It's almost nine and getting dark

And he tells me it's his fondest dream
To be on a Coatesville Little League Baseball team
To be like "the other guys, you know."
And I tell him that he cannot throw.

"You cannot throw. You cannot hit.
And you don't know baseball from shit.
And besides they have but little wit.
O Richie Holleran."

Ok, then I will reveal
How I, back then, did really feel.
Richie Halloran was my friend
And had told me of his coming end.

Joe Green

The doctors said that his dizzy spells
Meant he wasn't doing well.
And he heard his mom and dad
Crying. He said "I was so sad."

And his mom had told the nuns
Who had told the moms who had told their sons
Who considered him the Walking Dead.
"I want to be like those guys," he said.

So we were there in Central Park
Almost nine and getting dark.
"Christ, you're dumb" I did remark.
To Richie Holleran.

Another Christmas Poem

I don't know just how you feel
But I'd like to see the oxen kneel
Or even to hear the reindeer pause
And think "I'll bet it's Santa Claus."
But it's a not uncommon grief
To realize you have no belief
Since 10 when you think "I'll pass"
And are then dragged off to Midnight Mass
And on Christmas day must place a wreath
On a snowy tomb. You lack belief
That your mother's mother buried there
Is somehow winging through the air
In some celestial paradise.
You pretend to pray and watch the ice
Shining from a pine tree bough.
What is all this anyhow?
You can hear your heart and feel your breath
And everywhere is death, death, death.
Then in the car and to your aunt's
A skinny kid in baggy pants
Reading a book. It's Robin Hood!
And you would be there if you could
In the forest long ago
And Friar Tuck would say "Hey, Joe!
The King is come from long ago!
King Richard from across the sea!"
Who is mortal? It's not me.
And I'd laugh and pick up my longbow
Knowing where I had to go.
The snow would fall all that long night

Joe Green

And we would walk until the light
Can be seen there. There! Through the mist!
And all around. Ah, long the list
Robin, John and good old Will!
And the castle there upon the hill.
And my father drives and my mother smokes.
This is a world of horrible jokes:
You live and then one day you die.
You are mortal. So am I.
This was, perhaps, in '58
Not too early not too late
All years are always ever same
But, somehow, you always try to name
Who was there because they're gone
My dad is there. I see him yawn.
Always tired as you would be
If you sipped a daiquiri
Next to a giant Christmas tree
While my aunt smoking a Pall Mall
Complains the day is somewhat dull
And next day you again once more
Open up your little store
And wait for something and just wait
The year is Nineteen Fifty-Eight
And then we leave … and riding back
I remember seeing something black:
A shadow maybe in the woods
Maybe it was Robin Hood's
And above the world the moon!
I'd be leaving! Maybe soon.

The Ballad of Ernie White

I had a friend. His name it was Ernest.
Ernest fell into the mill blasting furnace
Chasing a home run. Fell over the fence.
I scored from first as Ernest went hence.
Our Field of Dreams was up on a hill
Directly above the Lukens steel mill.
Ernest was earnest. Man, he went after that ball!
They told his poor Mama he had a bad fall.
Ernest was earnest and, man, he was tense.
Exactly the guy to go over that fence.
We all felt quite proud and wondered how it would feel
To become instantly one with "Lukens' Finest Plate Steel."
"Let that be a lesson," my old Mama said.
I said that it would and went to my bed.
Life ain't no contest. Ain't no frabjulous journey.
Relax. Walk away. Remember poor Ernie.

Joe Green

Twilight Zone

It was '63 and I was alone.
Just my dog and me.
Watching *The Twilight Zone*.
Was it '63?

Watching Rod Serling
With his knowing grin.
He looked at me
Said "Joe, come in."

I turned the TV off
And the room was dark.
And my little dog
Began to bark.
Out in the hall
My shadow I saw.
I knew it was me
And that that would be all.

I saw my shadow
Come down the stairs.
I knew at once
I wasn't there.
I knew at once
I was nowhere.

So I turned the TV on.
Knew I would always be alone.

Somewhere nowhere
In the Twilight Zone.

Joe Green

Jipijapa Hat

The moon coach-and-foured it with its horrible lashery.
Saul Roth had implored it from Roth's haberdashery.
"Forty years out for business." Fought Death to a draw, so
Into the store walked Ricky Ricardo.

"Ricky Ricardo walked in. Bought a Jipijapa hat."
We didn't believe him. He was blind as a bat.
"Forty years out for business"
You can bet that, of course, all
The Roths didn't make it from the ghetto at Warsaw.

Moon beetles black dreidel indifferent very
Lashes Saul Roth to the Jew's cemetery.
"Ricky Ricardo walked in. Brought a Jipijapa hat."
Say it. You're happy. We didn't know about that.

The Diamond at the End of Time

A la carrera on the run again and the Federales
On my tail and I don't mean the Federales but
True hounds of Hell but I WAS in Mexico.
"Much madness is divinest sense" and it was
Me that said that though Shakespeare would never admit it
Following me around all the fucking time with his little notebook
And the Parker pen I gave him I mean he deserved it
Even though he took what the Hellhounds were after yeah
He had mojo and so there I was outside a little cantina
In Night of the Iguana country Senor Carrera to the Mexicans
And waiting … for what … but when you are looking
For the Diamond at the End of Time it might not matter
That Hellhounds are on your trail and you are drunk again.
Rock Drill. It does not cohere. On the third lunation.

They keep watch on the hilltops.
The moon was big and yellow and bleary so I was
Feeling fine and it was Midsummer and I was thinking
About Shakespeare take and take motherfucker
And the moon was big and you think I'm running again
The Black Zorro and then the moon winks at you
And you are someplace else and that's how it happens
Back in time or somewhen or somewhere. Man, I was
Just back from London 1590 or so I never checked
Exactly and it is so strange everyone you see there
On London bridge as you smell the stench everyone is dead
And you can't get that experience except by going
To a Republican convention but the stench is from the river.

Joe Green

I never thought Death had undone so many.
Another fine line of mine stolen but here I was
A black man in a white hat with a white feather and a silver suit
But they never gave me a glance onliest thing wrong
Was my bootheels were too low. They knew how to dress then
And there it was The Globe Theatre. Show out. Around Five
    O'Clock
In the Afternoon as it always is at times like these
When you are flung backward in time and you know
The little guy with the devil beard the ink stained
Wretch squatting outside the theatre trying to write something
With a goddamn quill as the Producer screams at him and he
Acts like he's someplace else his lips moving writing writing
Is the Bard himself. Mr William Shakespeare blotting
The Hell out of his lines and there is a tide in the affairs of men.

You got to catch it at the sticking point. It's like this
And I explained it to Shakespeare after I helped him out
With what to do when the bad guys got the drop
On the hero. You gotta have a distraction I told him
Christ don't you know that and the bad guys look away
And the hero grabs the sword and it's best if you have
A chandelier to swing from as he cries "Sa-thump whoreson
Hound taste cold steel!" and it's in his plays someplace
So I went right up to him and took his hat.
He jumped up. Shakespeare my man I said. Give me back
My hat and I am not your man he said and then when he looked
At me cried Amoor and I gave him back his hat and smiled
And said Yeah Love gets you into trouble I know
You got Dark Lady problems. But I ain't here for that!

Then I took out my Parker pen and said, This is for you

Yeah it's a pen try it and he did. Who are you he said
A free black man from the seacoast of Bohemia I told
Him and he didn't blink geography not being his strong suit
We gotta talk let's go man and he just nodded. We'll go to the
    Mermaid
You interest me strangely and I could tell it had happened to him
Before the deer stealing son of a bitch because he had
A little smile as he picked up his quill. You won't be needing
That anymore I said. You got a Parker pen there with endless ink
So don't try that shit on me. What do you know about the
    Diamond?
What Diamond? he said. That would be the Diamond at the
    End of Time.
Rock drill he said. Is Immortal Diamond he said.
Brother I said. He smiled. I said Let's be off to the Mermaid!
Fine Canary wine and the lascivious pleasings of a lute!

Milton stole that line. Shakespeare would have but he was
    sweating it
Like you do when you meet a free black man from the 20th
    century
Giving you a fine Parker pen with endless ink and some
Of your best lines. We got drunk first of course. Ben Jonson
Came in. What a damn bore but we didn't pay him no attention.
Ok I said you always callin' people whoresons in your plays, Bill
Why don't you just say motherfucker means the same thing
And he laughed and wrote it down and he admitted yes
He knew about the diamond and then the shadows seem to
Get more like real fucking scary shadows when he said
Alright I know Ezra Pound sent you he promised to come back!
I tried not to act scared. When was this? I asked and where?
Hsein he said Nova Vita. The Commonwealth.

That far shore at the Third Lunation. What the fuck does that
    mean?

I asked as I melted into the air.

Fool-begged, foolish-compounded, folly-fallen footlings foison
    plenty
Of flickering Flibbertigibbets, fluxive flouting-stock flewed as
Flax-wenches, fleering and flap-mouthed flirt gills and flesh
    mongers
Full-gorged yet frustrate. Pajocks and pantaloons you scream but
No one hears as you melt. The crystal fretting (CF) is fracted.
A certain ontological void is created. The exterior envelope is
    palpated to
Effect a hiatus in the lattice-work. Dehiscence or fission de facto
Of course always implicated and a liminal porosity but
    anticipated invagination of light
Delayed And the Da of Sa and the Non-place of Vorstellung
Temporarily inhibited by glissement all glockenspiel causing
The CF to groin glutted by vacuum awaiting glissando. You get
    pretty fucking tense
So no wonder all you want is a margarita and then another
And then another as you find yourself of all the gin joints in the
    world in a Mexican

Cantina where you have to take your tequila straight and
You know what you have what all hell wants which includes
Mr. Ezra Pound so you are outside of that cantina and it
    happens
Again. We go all darkling. You step out into darkness.
If I didn't want to die I wouldn't have lived and you know you
    are there

The Commonwealth. The far shore of the third lunation so, of
 course
There are black riders. There's just about anything in the
 Commonwealth
All Stories All sweet days. This is where you grew up if you
Were a certain kind of Kid so I knew where I was Midsummer
 Night's Dream
Woods Near Athens. Musick. Alone of us Ben Jonson said
Shakespeare would put an ass's head in Fairyland. And my black
 ass
Was there. Hell as they say could be Ilion Rome or any other
 town and
Even the woods behind Athens where right then two goblins got
 me
Ofays with SS insignia dragging me to a Castle a bleak wind
 rising.

Ah, bitter chill it was. Across the drawbridge. Stone and cold
 moon. Gargoyles.
And then into a room a lofty chamber triple arched the window
Candlelight, torchlight and they threw me down before the
 throne. Snarl
Of silver trumpet. They killed Keats! But no I see it is the Bard
 himself
Two goblin fuckers holding him and before me on the throne
 and stepping down
Mr. Ezra Pound himself. Ezra, you're a scholar, what's the time
 of day?
I say since it's important to confuse the motherfucker and
 maintain a high
And haughty style for that's the way it's written. You ready to be
 put in a cage?

Where is it? he says I want it and I will have it. It does not cohere
Which last I attribute to him being confused that a proud black man
Would have the Mojo. Which I did have which is why the hounds of Hell
Et cetera. Now you have to keep one step ahead of these evildoers so I
Took it out. You looking for this and I laughed to see him. Here's the Mojo.
Here's what you lookin for. Fix your poetry right up. Here it is.

Satchel pitching in Ponce de Leon Park against the Birmingham Black Barons
Threw the ball so motherfucking fast that it disappeared. And here it is Pound
But you don't know nothing about it. Here's the ball. Here's the Mojo you want
But you don't know nothin about it, do you? And Pound jumped back.
And the Nazi goblins jumped back. Whoa! Yes. Here it is and he couldn't say nothin'
But you know it is what it is when you see it. And Shakespeare was getting off of the floor as I told them all and threw the disappeared Satchel Paige ball up just a little
Smiling at them like the devil smiles looking Pound right in the eye thinking get
Up get up Shakespeare. Hsien. Rock Drill! You reading Frobenius, Benton, Del Mar
Aggassiz, Fenelolla knowing nothin about Ruth, Cool Papa Bell, The Splendid Splinter
Or the little guy sweating each pitch against class-D minor league semi-pros, thinking

St. Louis Stars, Detroit Wolves, Kansas City Monarchs,
    Homestead Grays, Pittsburgh Crawfords

Memphis Red Sox, Chicago American Giants, Kansas City
    Stars, Detroit Senators
Get up Shakespeare. Grover Cleveland Alexander sick and
    dying at Beaubier's Hotel
Get up your deer stealing fuck. All over all over. You never even went to a Yankees Game and you want the mojo? Here take it and I wound up and threw the ball at Pound
Ran at the goblins, faked, got their swords flipped one to the Swan of Avon sword glittering in the torchlight cried I was born to this motherfuckers and of course
The torches guttered up with a goblin flame a hot wind from
    Hell blew into the chamber
And who should leap out from behind the arras but more coldly
    grinning Nazi shitheels
Saw Shakespeare cut down two of them howling Angels and Ministers of Grace defend Us! Ha Ha I laughed We gotta do it ourselves and the disappeared ball of course back
In my pocket mojo working Shakespeare and I back to back grinning as darkness surrounds us and what should we do against it but leap on the chandelier swing to the
Tower winding stairs kicking Pound on the head rush like
    happy ghosts up the dark
Stairs making it to the great door and shutting it just in time.
    All Hell pounding.

Remember this when you write *Macbeth* I panted. Knock
    Knock Knock on the gate
A great effect no don't try to write it down and we were on the
    ramparts Hell's Agents

Pounding at the door. That fuckers gonna break I warned him. The clouds blowing across the moon darkness surrounds us and then I saw it the star the greeny star
Winking in the west low there right over the trees. I pointed to it as the door began breaking We can't hold em off Shakespeare screamed. I looked round the ramparts Hey a great place for some Prince's fathers ghost to walk o' nights I told him just trying to calm him down. Look at that star. That greeny star. We going there. He was too scared. Look up I shouted at him for the wind was blowing now and shadows comin' down from the moon. We're gonna go there and my mojo will get us there. What the fuck are you talking about you crazy black bastard? he screamed. I grabbed him took him to the edge of the ramparts 300 feet up and they had broken through the door.

Jump I screamed Jump like Butch and Sundance! Whooped!
    Grabbed the Bard and we jumped into the dark!

All the Federales say, they could of had him any day.
They only let him slip away, out of kindness I suppose. I'm Pancho I shouted and you my man are Lefty cause we floated away into
    that
Dark me waving at the goblins floating toward that greeny star
And I got the ball and threw it right up whoosh felt a little sick and
We were there I looked down the green diamond and of course
Remembering how I first walked into Connie Mack stadium with
    my daddy
Seeing the diamond green and eternal always remember my
    daddy said
We were at The Diamond at the End of Time! I knew right away.
We stood there in the stands. The Diamond at the End of Time
    shone below us. It was

The fifth inning of the 1932 World Series. Number 3, Babe Ruth, was at bat. Charlie Root was pitching. The Babe pointed to center field. I shouted
That's the Babe and that's the Called Shot. Watch! And we watched as Root hurled the fastball that Ruth hit high high and out of here to forever!

The Called Shot—the immortal moment of baseball.

The Diamond at the End of Time.

We were alone in the stands except for a hunched seated figure not far away in a tan raincoat I recognized him at once. It was God. He was God! That's God I told the Bard. Oh, shit the Bard said It's true. God's a Yankee fan. How the hell did he know about baseball? The Babe headed for home and there was Lou Gehrig ready to shake his hand. The Iron Horse! Man this is great. I said Cool Papa Bell did that kind of shit all the time. You never hear about it though. And Gehrig is at bat and hits another Home run! The thunder after the lightning! Then it happened all over again. Again the Babe raised his hand indicating strike two and again he stood out of the batter's box and pointed a finger at center field and hit a tremendous smash 436 feet over the fence and Into a ticket booth at Waveland and Sheffield Avenues and again he rounded the field holding up four fingers now and the Iron Horse was up to bat and again smashed the ball into Eternity. And then it all happened again

What's s the matter with God I asked?

And I knew God is trapped watching beauty over and over and
    over.

It was 1932.

Goddamn it! I shouted He's watching while the Nazis are taking over.

Again it happened. God stood up and looked over at us. He looked sad standing there surrounded by empty beer bottles. We went over. Me and Shakespeare.

He looked at me. Gimme the ball he said so I flipped it to him. He flipped it back to Shakespeare standing there grinning with his little devil beard.

God gave me a box of crackerjacks. Nice to have met you Dooley Shakespeare said. Tossed the ball up caught it and disappeared I really didn't say everything I said God said and later I remembered Yogi Berra had said that and the next thing I knew I was outside of Wrigley Field It was 1932. Chicago. God was not watching here.

Hitler and all that and me just standing.

It, of course, began to rain.

And I knew why I was the Loneliest Ranger.
Knew again why I was the Loneliest Ranger.
God gone. The Nazis closing in. And Shakespeare had my mojo.

Finis.

—*The Loneliest Ranger*

The Ballade of Susie Lamont

Some talk of Hegel. Some of Kant.
But permit me to speak of Susie Lamont
Who jumped for the Frisbee and there in the air
Was eternally present with no underwear.
This was in the Sixties. I was at Marquette.
By the bones of St. Thomas I see her yet.
She taught me so much of becoming and being.
"Help me Aristotle I can't believe what I'm seeing!"
And she was much sweeter than Hegel and Kant
So much more demure was Susie Lamont.
It happened so fast. The moment soon passed
Of Becoming and Being revealed.
Then she went away with her boyfriend Ray
And left me alone in the field.
Oh that very day I took the philosopher's way
Went home alone as per plan
And for the rest of the day wrote a boring essay
That ended with three words: "What is Man?"
About "Oh what the loss is that the world is in process!"
And I cited Teilhard de Chardin.

1968

Mary said "I have a plan.
I'm reading Teilhard De Chardin."
I can't remember what she said
When I suggested Alfred North Whitehead.
We were high on LSD
And I was happy that she spoke to me.
Jimi Hendrix was on the wall
And she seemed so frail and small
And trembled. Outside it snowed.
She said she hated *On the Road*
Went out in the snow with her boyfriend, Jack.
Always remember "Don't look back."
Next year I heard that she was dead.
In a car accident they said.
For what it's worth she's ever here
In the trembling noösphere.

Go Tell the Achyans

Go tell the Achyans
That here obedient to their wish we lie.
Or something like that.
I remember
Drizzle in Coatesville
Meeting Kevin outside the Bongo.
Always smoking then.
"That rich bitch Lucy McIlvane
Jumped off the bridge at Exton."
Looking around
For the police.
"She was high on acid.
Here it is."
"Something to do with her name,"
I said. And Kevin laughed.
Probably sold it to her.
We didn't want to remember.
But I do now.
A PINK! VW.
"Slow down." Her grinding the gears.
Talking about meeting the Panthers.
Her blue veined hand. Small girl.
Fluttering. "Read *Catcher in the Rye*
At least 20 times," she said.
Asking about Kevin, Gary, Steve.
"Kevin's in California last I heard.
Gary joined the Marines.
How about that?"
Nervous girl.
Falling.

Joe Green

No one to catch her.
Thirty (More!) years later.

Go tell the Achyans.
Whatever that should mean.

Kevin Anent Jimi

December 31, 1969
I am on the train to NYC
To visit my friend Kevin
Who, a few years too
Late for San Francisco,
Moved there. Going
To the Jimi Hendrix New Year's Eve
Concert (With the "Sounds of East Harlem")
And you can read about it as I did
Only yesterday in a very nice
Coffee table kind of book
On the Fillmore East.

Finding his walk-up flat
(He called it that) going in
Two of his friends there
Maybe Five in the afternoon
In any case and Kevin
Shooting up smack

I say "Kevin I am
Fucking appalled." maintaining
A certain distance as I did
From all that looking at
His arm (now gone, nothing at all)
And he grinning then sighing.

Wake up let's go and somehow
We do. I have the tickets
The Sounds of East Harlem first

Joe Green

Kevin nodding and then
Bill Graham introducing
Jimi and Kevin is awake
And then the man is there!

Looks out can't see.

An instant before he starts Kevin
Leaning forward and I say
"You keep doing that shit
You'll be dead in two years."

"Man," Kevin says, "Shutup
Can't you ever be serious?"

I Love Them Old Hippies

I love them old hippies. The kind like before.
Like my poor old friend Kevin who slept on my floor
Who told me he wouldn't be sick anymore
But went back to the streets in the morning.
Saying "You know you're in trouble and you got the blues
When you forgot all you learned from *Mother Earth News*."
"I'm going to Mexico. Sleep under the stars."
He went down to Mexico. Found many fine bars
Where he could drink down the night and forget about wars
And wake up in the desert in the morning.
"I'll tell you what Dooley. I'm not going to stay.
I'm going to New York instead of L. A.
With my Carmelita. Our love will abide."
But they lost it to junk on the Lower East Side.
The water is waly. The water is wide.
I got a call early one morning.
Now, my poor friend Kevin's gone down to the dark.
His VW bus is in permanent "Park."
He'd talk until morning then light up a Lark
And tell me he believed in transcendence.
"You know you're in trouble and you got the blues
When you forgot all you learned from *Mother Earth News*."

Joe Green

A Ballade

The Vietnam War was going on
And I was at Fort Hood
Sometimes feeling pretty sad.
Most times pretty good.

I'll sing of soldiers in the rain
And how it's sometimes pretty hard
And tell you how it was so strange
On Tank Destroyer Boulevard.

I reported to the Orderly Room
To good old Major Moore.
Who said to me "Godammit, son
Why don't you close the door?"

I about faced and about faced
Then Major Moore put on his hat.
Said "Sergeant Green, I'm leaving now
Don't let out the cat."

I stood there in amazement.
He said, "That cat talks in Latin.
He pretty mean and crazy
And his name is General Patton."

Now, I know the General Reader
Will cry out sans belief.
But Major Moore strode out that door
With his secret grief.

He had just returned from Vietnam
And was thinking "Fuck the Army."
And he was not the only one.
All of us were barmy.

Major Moore went out the door
To his Buddha garden.
The Buddha looted from Saigon
When Major Moore was parting.

He had two guys assigned just there
To care for the flowers and trees.
You don't believe me? I don't care.
This was the Seventies.

I went back to the Orderly Room
Right up to the company clerk.
"Jesus Christ what is my doom?
Where do I go for work?"

The company clerk stopped typing.
Said, "Here, take a look at this."
It was a novel he was writing
Entitled *The Last Kiss*.

"It's set in 1984
When everyone is dead
Except for a boy and his little dog."
That's really what he said.

He looked at me inquiringly
As he adjusted his toupee.

Joe Green

He was a Mormon and a novelist
And, quite bitterly, was gay.

And he played fine jazz piano
In a melancholy way.

Yes, he played fine jazz piano
In a melancholy way.

I read the page and looked at him
And pronounced the writing fine.
He perked right up. Said, "My name is Jim.
Do you really like the final line?"

I looked at Jim quite closely
And felt that I had no choice
And said in a voice quite ghostly
"It makes me think of Joyce."

Then I picked up my duffel bag
And headed out the door
And I seemed to hear a Joplin rag
As I saw who I stood before.

It was Sergeant Major Gilmore Davis
Who said, "Boy, put down your gear
And go back and get a pair of pliers
And bring them over here."

Sergeant Major Gilmore Davis!
In his Gilmore Davis way

Had a face like "Jesus Save Us!"
But a smile like Sugar Ray.

Last days in Army service
He'd been in since '44.
And you'll think he might be nervous
With all the shit he did endure:

World War Two and then Korea.
Three tours of Vietnam.
But you have the wrong idea.
He was mellow. He was calm.

He took the pliers. Said, "Come with me."
We went to the Rec room.
Where he adjusted the TV
Until Nat King Cole began to croon.

"Stay here, boy" he said to me.
But he didn't mean it meanly.
"After Andy Williams.
We'll watch *I Dream of Jeannie.*"

I went out into the Fort Hood night
With my gear upon my shoulder
Humming "Mama, It's Alright."
I had a chance of getting older.

I was there near the Second Armor
And the First Cavalry
A screw-up in a lost brigade
In a Lost Company.

Joe Green

The Cobras shivered above us.
The tanks drove down the road.
And left us alone. God loved us.
Just like he loved Tom Joad.

I got assigned to language school
To that strange faculty
Or draftees, drunks and derelicts
Teaching deportees:

Wives brought back to the USA
From Korea and Vietnam
From little villes and long lost hills
From Seoul and from Saigon.

So they could work in restaurants
Or dance in topless clubs
And smoke opium in trailers
And give those fine "back rubs."

One day Captain Thomas
Came looking for his wife.
"Where's that gook bitch? I'll kill her!"
Then he took his life.

And she got all of his insurance.
She had quite a business sense.
And opened up a pawnshop
With Sergeant Gilkey, hence

Her marriage to the Sergeant
Which followed hard upon

The orders Sergeant Gilkey
Got to go to Vietnam.

And when he was listed missing
And then he turned up dead.
She said "I was always lucky lucky."
And then was quickly wed

To the guy across the street
Who had the Army Surplus store.
If you don't find that just and meet
It's what this country's for.

She was in my English class
Before these sad events.
It was time for her to give a speech
And she seemed somewhat tense.

"I was at the movie.
On Tet. We in Saigon.
Big noise. Scream everywhere.
Go up a big bomb.

Kill everyone. My mother!
My mother, my sister died."
She looked at me and then sat down
And never never cried.

And I remember young John Kostovich.
He was from Chicago.
He had a Ford Econo—Hippie van
With the usual strange cargo.

Joe Green

On one side was the Peace Sign.
On the other side a frog
And underneath that was the line
"Onward through the Fog!"

He drove that van to Mexico
And came back with some grass.
He told me, "Joe, I wanted to just go.
They all can kiss my ass."

And I remember him a year from then
On the phone. I heard him scream.
"My brother got killed in Fucking 'Nam."
It all seems like a dream.

He ran right out. Got in the van.
Screaming all the way.
Jim Linden said to me
"Do you think he'll be ok?"

He got a "compassionate discharge."
And then in '71
I got a letter: "I'm living large.
Up here in Oregon."

The real war was still going on.
Then Sergeant Davis said "You losers.
Grab your packs and get your guns.
We're going on maneuvers."

I was in charge of our two squads.
Prayed "God, I thee implorest.

Enlighten all the little gods
To get us lost inside the forest."

I told my guys, "We'll need a lot of beer
For this goddamn fake war
And guitars and books and a lot of grass.
What are you waiting for?"

So we drove off in our Army truck
And I did not feel bereft.
Said "Damn, I can't believe our luck."
When they turned right then we turned left.

The real war was still going on.
The fake war did not alarm us.
I lounged outside in the Texas sun
In my Grateful Dead pajamas.

I had brought along Ulysses.
Joyce was always such a charmer.
But I lounged outside in that Texas breeze
Reading Philip Jose Farmer.

And that night Tom played his guitar
Beneath the Texas moon
So far away from the real war.
"Lay Down Your Weary Tune."

"Lay down your weary tune, lay down,
Lay down the song you strum,
And rest yourself 'neath the strength of strings
No voice can hope to hum."

Joe Green

Thirty years ago and more.
Some are dead. All to me are gone so long.
What in hell was all that for?
I end this weary song.

"Lay down your weary tune, lay down,
Lay down the song you strum,
And rest yourself 'neath the strength of strings
No voice can hope to hum."

The Ballad of Little Noddy

Up the magic mountain
Down the rushy glen
We daren't go a-hunting
For fear of little men.

Little Kants and Hegels
Socrates and Platos
Pissing in our garden
Eating our tomatoes.

Preaching their philosophy
To prove their very piss is
The cockleshell theosophy
Of Hermes Trismegistus.

Once there was a little boy
Little Noddy was his name
Who held on to his little joy
Beneath his counterpane.

What a pretty wanton boy
Slaughtering the flies
And spattering the bourgeoisie
In their dogmatic stys!

What a brave young Nimrod!
Who with lists prefers to hunt
For Consciousness and Cabbages
Coelacanths and Cunt.

Joe Green

Vile rumor states our lad avers
All three the same dish
But Rumor's wrong: "I much prefer
The last sans consciousness.

I am a carefree deliquant!

Will take a cabbage everyday
Though Coelacanths are elegant
When in a family way.
I prefer the simple vegetable

Much before another.
Its inner silk suggestible
Of my late lamented mother.
Picture a silken draped boudoir

And Daddy behind the arras
The cabbage in a pink peignoir
And certain scents from Paris
Daddy chained and gagged. O! Rare!

And a slit for him to see
And another in the cabbage dear
Just big enough for me.
Then I caress the vegetable

And read her Havelock Ellis
And poetry pansexual
Of the dying on the trellis
Of many a time-blown rose

Wailing for her demon lover
And many a well-blown nose
Ever waiting for another
Finger than the one it loves!

A nose whose passion lingers
Stars above—though penetrated nightly
By the finger it abhors.
Until the turf lies lightly, lightly

And the doors, the golden doors
Of Eternity open!
And the dear digit it adores
d
e
s
c
e
n
d
s
All Beatrice to its bosogger.
And then I take my daddy's Luger
This is how my daddy wooed her
And then, and then! I leap! I leap!
Ravaging that cabbage
With a passion so steep
It o'ertops Dante's!

And then I calm her
With a murmured verse *von*
Jeffery Dahmer.

Joe Green

Daddy thinks the cabbage mother
Daddy's always getting thinner
Though every night he has another
Piece of mother for his dinner."

You can see that little Noddy
Had quite eccentric passions
Perhaps banal to anybody
Who keeps up with the fashions:

Vile poetry and matricide
A bit of old Jocasta
A weariness of time and tide
And, to make the moment last

A burning in a gemlike flame
Of all of his relation.
But he is like the gentle rain
The leaders of a nation

Direct ten million tons of bombs
Upon the place beneath
Bunkers, bridges, dads, and moms!
Roll me over Lethe!

Our little Noddy after all
Is rather ineffectual
His sins are white and do appall
But, at least, not intellectual.

All passion spent he rests his cheek
And recites a soothing psalm

And, perhaps, he dreams of leeks
But the vision of napalm

Is sugar plums and marzipan
To those across the sea
Who calculate the body count
Sing "Nearer my God to thee.

Nearer to thee Lord!" Then they
Adjust their calculations
And (100,000 say)
Are gone
gone
gone
Quite away.

And then, they face the tribulations
Of dog shit in Harvard Yard.
(Professor Booby's Lhaso Apso again)

Many miles away
The General says:
"Men, here is you mission. We want numbers!"
Arise ye nations from your dogmatic slumbers!!

In a geste most incandescent
The jungle algebras luminescent.
The mother, child, and sturdy peasant
All become quite deliquescent.

Flowing in a fiery stream!
Flowing in a golden dream!

Joe Green

Till they arrive at Harvard Yard
Where Booby thinks it a canard
"That's not my dog's shit in Harvard Yard.
Not my dog's shit in Harvard Yard.

The priest, the King, the simple clown.
Intellectual vileness trickles down.

As does this verse. O comic Muse
Make my bowels and bladder swell!
Jesus Christ, I've paid my dues.
Deliver me to Infidel.
Who is not a little Noddy.
Little Noddy's anybody.

Souls of poets dead and gone
Be sure to keep your condoms on.
Be advised your lissome muse
Won't be as prankish as she used.
And though, perhaps, your stiffened chillness
Will seem to some a formal stillness
And the worm your daily wage is:
You'll still be better than John Cage is.

Ah, she's back. My verse becomes more regular.
Except for that last line. A rhyme! A rhyme!
Hey, Tim the keg-u-la
You bought is all drunk up.

That's a lie.
He isn't even here.
Hasn't been for a year.

I loved him best.
We were the "Owl Oak Press"
He had three wives and a silver star.
And killed himself in Carmel, Ca.
1/1/91

Car
Car
Car

the cars said.

Did it the American way. In his car with a .45.
The word I want to rhyme is "alive."
Alive! Alive O!
Silver stars, and wars and wars,
And pretty maids all in a row.

O Tim! You lost your town the race.
But at least you found a parking space.

Alas, poor Tim is not no body
Let's go back to Little Noddy.

One night little Noddy
Maddened by the crowds
Who danced the limbic limbo
'Neath the Magellanic clouds

Went up the magic mountain
And down the rushy glen

Joe Green

And by St. Tommy's fountain
He met the little men!

O see their vile symposium
Underneath the trees
A cacophile colloquium
Of venal venomy.

Buboes like bijous!
Transcendent logorrheas
Blood or beetlejuice
On their paideas.

Socrates accouchant
Plato on his knees
Hegel only kegeled
While Kant begged, "Please."

Poor panting pooh-bahs
And moon-botched mulattoes
Hear the ontic *ohh ahs*
In their secret grottos

The very meager spewing
The sudden going slack
The strangled senseless mooing.
I want my money back.

Poor Noddy thought them pixies
A typical cathexis
With many a cunning lick he
Sought logosrhythmic nexus.

"O fondle all my fabula
Make my bowels go whoosh
Bite my incunabula
Gerbil my cartouche!"

They crowned him then with laurel
And pulled his undies down
And had a little quarrel
About quintessence brown

And who would have the precedent
And who would wait behind
But in concord incrudescedent
They chose symbol over sign.

First they gave him No-Doz
And then they bound his arms
Then spoke to him of Logos
And of his manly charms

Then they put him in a toga
And in the best Platonic forms
Whispered he was deathless
And buggered him in swarms

Drizzled him with powdered gold
And decked his dick with lapis
Diddled with his tiny fold
And called him "Dear Priapus."

Filled his behind with sea-dark wine
And then they crammed the ice in

Joe Green

"How do you feel?" "Why I feel fine,
Rather Dionysian."

Then they took a silver spoon
And scraped him out all hollow.
He laughed and bayed right at the moon
"I feel just like Apollo."

Then they stroked his little bum
(It really was quite flexible)
And gashed a hole between his legs
Until he wasn't very sexable.

See the timeless golden dial!
Hear the crystal spheres!
See the unmoved crocodile
Cry his pearly tears!

The good, the true, the beautiful
A frenzy fine and flighty
And Noddy shouts, "O! take me! Do!
I feel like Aphrodite."

Plato did and him y-thrid.
"Dear master, are you peeing?"
"It's just the God you silly sod.
You're just becoming being."

Let's leave him there. O my dear Muse
I must say that I detest
The words that I am forced to use
Like "bugger" and the rest

And pee and fuck and dick and cunt
(Poor Noddy's vade mecum)
But I only sing as he was wont
Which is, it seems, "fair dinkum"

Or whatever they say near Botany Bay
In the land of Noddy's fellows,
Australia the Fair! And, anyway
Even old Catullus

And a murder thick of other bards
Were forced to this vile usage.
Don't ask me who. It's rather hard
Living in a loose age

Where buggery is thought a crime
(I mean the kind consensual)
While helping thousands out of time
Is reaching your potential.

Sing mea culpa everyone
Pick up the muse and lug her
Guts to the top of Helicon
And bugger, gently, bugger.

Sweet Christ! Not yet! Unhand her, Mark
It's a swerving so to swive
We're still on Wilson River Drive
And Noddy's still alive.

He guards the sacred oxen
The oxen of the Sun.

Joe Green

But a glamour seems to mock him.
He only sees the one.

And this one looks just like a cow.
So what does Noddy dare?
"Flossie my own *fleur du mal*!"
Then he goes all Baudelaire.

And takes her in unnatural ways
Ways so vile and low
They were unmatched until the days
Of Verlaine and Rimbaud.

The cow just mooed and chewed and mooed.
Noddy did what should be banned.
O depths of Moral Turpitude!
He mentioned old Ayn Rand!

He only muttered out the word
To try to keep from coming
He was dreaming of the pliant herds
And of his different drumming.

The cow cried out! The levin flashed!
Noddy screamed in pain.
The cow dissolved! The levin flashed!
Little Noddy came.

What against he couldn't tell
But it was the Goddess Io
Who had simply been through hell.
You can read it in her bio.

Noddy struggled to get off
And gave a little cry-a
The goddess gave a little cough
"They call the wind Mariah.

The fire is Tess, the rain is Joe
I hope I get this straight.
Apollo has a golden bow.
Aphrodite's always late.

Zeus has the juice and just hangs loose
Hera's such a hassle.
And I learned the truth from Lenny Bruce
That Plato is an asshole."

The goddess felt a tiny pinch
And touched her sacred portal
Little Noddy dared not flinch
"I think I smell a mortal."

And then she felt a nasty itch
In the derrière direction.
"Oh dear," she sighed "This is a bitch
I've got a yeast infection.

A douche might work. A douche divine.
Of amaranth and rue
And equal parts of turpentine
And a little Mountain Dew."

She sighed and wished. Behold the douche!
A boiling viscous fluid

That chuckled like a Scaramouche
In a cunning little cruet.

"Douche to the Gods, my lady fair,"
The douche cried with panache
Made little Fairbanks in the air
And fondled his moustache.

But what of Noddy? Damn my eyes.
I seem to have forgotten.
He hung there by a mild surmise
And smelled like fish most rotten

Behold! The douche leaps from the cup
And quivers on the quim.
Noddy weeps and covers up
And sings an English hymn

A quavering tune: "I thee implore
To save a wretch like me."
That Little Noddies like to sing
When far away at sea

And their mothers are so far away
And it's really dark at night
And it's a long way to Bristol Bay
With that nasty bosun tight.

But the douche just laughed and tried to peer
Through the deific tangle
He was a jolly musketeer
Who held his sword a-dangle

That sword had killed a thousand yeasts
From Moscow to Peoria
And drank the blood of judas priests
All for the greater glory....

"Ah", he cried when he saw the lad
This is to damn too damn too damn bad
And the douche just wept: "Sad sad sad
This is just too damn too damn too damn bad."

And little Noddy wept. He knew the truth.
His only friend was a goddamn douche.
The douche heaved a heavy sigh.
"All of this will pass."

And picked up a crab just passing by
Who bit Noddy in his ass.
"Free at last," the poor boy squeaked
Unstuck from his own jism

And saw where his becoming leaked
All sparkling like a prism.
He reached his hand around behind
And plucked out the owl feather

Preferring matter over mind
Started running for the heather.
The Goddess laughed and saw him run
(It really wasn't fair)

"A mortal. Oh, what jolly fun."
Then seemed to catch the air.

Joe Green

Little Noddy shrieked and fell
And cried out (rather quizzical)

"Jesus Christ this hurts like hell
My dick is metaphysical!"
And so it was! It dangled there
At least ten or twenty versts
What once was meat was passing rare.

God knows how that hurts.
That mini-length of Oscar Mayer
Now thinner than the thistle
Upon the head of Richard Pryor

Or Nancy Reagan's pistle
Stretched out in far flung molecules
Like a St. Tommy's angel band
One end near his follicles

The other in her hand!
She reeled him back and played with him
Like a fish upon a string.
He'd make a pretty pendant

She could even make him sing.
Poor Noddy begged and sobbed and moaned
As he dandled twixt her breasts
He bitched and kvetched and groaned and groaned

Till the goddess got depressed.
She took the little mannikin

And held him up to see
"I once knew a Mick named Finnigan

That sounded just like thee.
What do you want you little shit?"
Then Noddy did reply
"I want this terrible dream to quit

If not, I want to die."
The goddess sighed and twitched her nose
The little guy was free!
He ended up upon the ranch
With Hoss and Pa and me.
He's happy now cause all he does
He does it all for Lorne.
And what a wiz he was he was
Shucking all the corn.
He talks philosophy with Hoss
Does his oriental thing
Bitches and bemoans his loss
And buggers poor Hop Sing!

The little men? Why she found them.
In their tiny elfin grot.
And listened to their boring talk
Screwed up her nose, said "NOT!"
And they were changed, changed udderly
To ugly leprechauns
And, though they are more cuddderly,
They'll still fuck up your lawns
And bugger moths and butcher flies
As they were wont to do

Joe Green

And fashion little priestly stys
All in the morning dew
They'll "crucify the butterflies"
"Break gnats upon the wheel."
Then tell you with a wild surmise,
"I guess it's how we feel."

Four and twenty blackbirds
Eat the ever-dying swan
Tiresius eats Jesus
All bloody flows the Don
Aristotle in his bottle
Keeps looking for a ship
But tiny sailors sail away
And let the big seas slip.

Straight for the heart of Lyra.

"I'm so pleased we're not dining at the ranch tonight.
Hop Sing's such a filthy cook."
—Peter O'Toole

"Was he more convinced of the esthetic value of the spectacle? Indubitably in consequence of the reiterated examples of poets in the delirium of the frenzy of attachment or in the abasement of rejection invoking ardent sympathetic constellations or the frigidity of the satellite of the planet."
—James Joyce, *Ulysses*

Jim Moore

Major Moore isn't any more
As he said
Sitting in the Buddha Garden.
Our C.O. 529th MI Company
Fort Hood, Texas
Just off Tank Destroyer Boulevard
And he was our King.
One time, years later, when I went to Thailand
Leaving the airport and flowers everywhere
My cab driver said "It's the King's Birthday!"
And I felt fine like I was in Fredonia
A comic opera country but with Emerald Buddha
And Jade Buddha and Golden Buddha
And thought of old Major Moore and how
Something had happened to him
When he was in Thailand back then.
Liason to the Air Force
Helping them discover just what 50 miles
Of the Ho Chi Minh trail that they would obliterate that day.
Major Moore was a West Point man
And a "I don't wear the ring, anymore." man
Who came back from Thailand with "Pat"
Whose real name was something like Pattypat Pattypat.
And who knows what happened it was
Anna and the King of Siam only backward
And she shimmered there in Texas
As he addressed us.
"Men," he said. "Men, I feel that I am
As good as any of you." And paused.
"And that you are as good as me."

And waved his hand at Sergeant Gonzalez
Who said "Company! Dismissed!"
In a wry baritone. One year to retirement.
"Wait," Major Moore said.
"Men, I bought ten copies of this book
Stranger in a Strange Land and they'll
Be in the orderly room and I'd like each of you
to read it. And think about it. Dismissed!"
What happened is this.
Our XO was Lieutenant Hanson
A ROTC man from Texas
And a snake.
June in the Buddha Garden.
"Major Moore is no more," Jim Moore said.
Disgraced. Dismissed. Branded.
"Have you ever read Vonnegut?"
And he was gone to—really—Fawn Grove Pa.
Where he and Pat had a few kids
And he pondered The Strawberry Alarm Clock
And never killed himself.
Lieutenant Hanson was also gone.
Within three months.
During a field exercise someone set up his tent
Right over a nest of copperheads
And he blew off his foot trying to shoot them.
Don't look at me. I didn't do it.

ARA KILLIJIAN

Ara Killijian read William Saroyan
But nobody ever caught him.
"Just a book I have."
We all need our secrets—or needed anyway
Stuck there between the First Cav
(Napalm in the morning!)
And the 2nd Armored Division—
Actually commanded by George Patton Jr.
So we understood when Ara went crazy.
And walked around everywhere
Arms outstretched like the crucified Christ
Asking everybody "What is the number one?"
It was, at least, original but
He would get in your way
When you were, for example, smoking
In the Buddha garden thoughtfully provided
by Major Moore. Buddhas looted from who cares.
"What is the number one?"
"Shut the hell up, Killijian. Take it someplace else."
So we were somewhat startled when
He jumped off the top of the barracks
And got killed.
"He really was crazy," we said.
And I remember Jim Linden said
"I wonder what the number one really is?"
Flicked his cigarette to the ground
And went to the movies.

Joe Green

Fort Dix

"You can go to the movies in groups of six."
The old sergeant says. I am at Fort Dix
Just after basic. A General Alarm:
Fort Dix is overrun by guys back from Vietnam.
"What crap," I thought. And walked on down the hill.
The army says "Don't do this." I say "I will."
Go with one other. Some guy named Sam.
Who tells me he can't wait to go to Vietnam.
From some town in Ohio. Maybe Martins Ferry.
At least I hope. Man I am very
Interested to see what I can see. Strange days.
I would see what I could see anyways!
I don't know what the hell I mean by this
Something about Fate. Whatever this THIS is.
New to me and caught up … and here am I.
From Here to Eternity crossed with *Catcher in the Rye*
Unreal just then so I go … why ever tarry?
Go with a nitwit from Ohio to see *Dirty Harry*.
And slump up from my seat in my most insouciant manner
To stand ironically for the "Star Spangled Banner."
The audience—Jesus Christ—all stoned or drunk
They cheer and cheer. "Do you feel lucky, punk?"
I don't. Leave. Go back and lie in my bunk.
Asking myself all night: "Do you feel lucky, do you feel lucky

… Punk?"

Where Are You Now Charlie Solomon?

Dear Charlie,
Last night I dreamed that you were dead
Which you won't mind since I haven't heard of you in more than
 thirty years
And there's no way you'll read this if you are living
And if you're dead I'm sure you have other things to do
If my dream was right. I had to dream I had woken up to be sure
 it was

You ... Charlie Solomon looking yeah I'm sorry like Ratso Rizzo
Which I assured you you didn't look like you were so broken
 hearted about it.
That was when ... in the Seventies sometime which is just about
 as precise
As we get up here in Yellowknife. '72 maybe or at least since
I remember you aspired to a 1971 Volkswagen Super Beetle
Just something you said when you showed me the radio telescope
 you

Had built out behind your trailer in Bisbee Arizona about a month
Before you disappeared—for me—forever.
So in my dream I saw you in the crowd of ghosts in the night air
The Christmas night air I saw through the window. Dreaming
 that
Scene from *A Christmas Carol* (the book) Marley backing away
as the window opens "I wear the chains I forged in life!" and then
 gone

And me in my Scrooge nightgown and cap rushing to the window
And seeing the spirits trying to trying to save someone (a little girl!

A sad man!) but helpless and you gave me a little wave you had
A top hat and cane and looked damn dapper and were watching
    it all

And somehow I was Bill Murray and made a goofy wry remark
    (the movie)
Which I forget maybe something about how they didn't get you.
Back at Fort Huachuca 1970-something and I was new and had
To stay in the barracks for a month or two and you were on the
    upper bunk
When I dropped my duffel bag and man knowing what I know
    now
I should have been happy that I had a guy who looked like Ratso
    Rizzo

And was taking a correspondence course in witchcraft.
"Who isn't crazy these days?" I would have said to all those stories.
I can appreciate it now. Up here in Yellowknife you're what we
    need.

"Yeah? Let me tell you about Charlie Solomon. That guy was
    crazy.
He got drafted in '65 or something right out of high school.
They were taking anybody—even Charlie—and they were
    keeping them.

Charlie must have been busted twice in his first two years and
They let him re-enlist and the he was busted twice more.
You know what for? Ok, this is true. Charlie was working in
    supply
And he found out—he read everything—from some old papers
    that

Our MI Company in WW2 was entitled to a railroad car.
So he ordered one. Months later the Company Commander got
    a call....

But Charlie was sincere and everybody knew it.
So all they did was bust him to Private again.
Sincerity counted for a lot in the old army.
There was always a place for a sincere fuckup.
Which is the way things should be.
And let me tell you he was sincere. Huachuca was the
    headquarters of

The Army Electronic warfare center so while Charlie was
    ordering
That railroad car he was also borrowing everything he needed
To build a radio telescope to detect aliens which Charlie
    sincerely
Thought were a menace or had to be watched in any case and
This also required him to build a headquarters out in the desert
Where he spent weekends. A broken-down trailer near Bisbee
With orange shag carpeting and electronic manuals and
    soldering irons

And the damn telescope thing beeped which was good enough
    for me.

By then following the rule that the army did then
That there was always a place for a sincere fuckup
Charlie had been removed from supply and given a job
As the clerk in the Classified Document depository where
As he told us he read all about the secret experiments the
    Russians

Were conducting with child psychics at an undisclosed place
Below the Siberian tundra who were sending out their astral
    bodies
Or what we in our ignorance called astral bodies to peek into
Kissinger's secret meetings or so we suspected."
You were happy then, Charlie.

But I'll bet you were even happier when
After getting orders to Vietnam you vanished from
The face of the earth but were sincere enough
To send back the secret documents you had taken
To Colonel Whateverhisnamewas with that little note.
"Enjoyed reading these"
Exactly as you wrote that.
You must have been happy.

Where are you now Charlie Solomon?

Oh, My

September 30, 1968
The *New Jersey* was bombarding the DMZ
But what the hell did we know about that
And even grey-eyed Pallas Athene
So far away from home?

We were in Quang Tri province
Right or someplace like that and
Had taken a lot of casualties.

Flying in and that was when
Wars were really fucked up.
And just 20 years ago and now?
And all that jive doesn't have the
Same whatever.

You know.... Used to be you would be sitting
In a bar someplace and you would
Hear them.... all those names like poetry
Pleiku, An Khe, Ban Me Thuot
LZ Blackhawk, LZ Hardtimes
Happy Valley, Phu Cat
And the guys they always look like the same
At least to you ... and the stories ...

"We were in Quang Tri which
Is up north and we were in
The bush and nervous—an ambush
Remember the claymores said
This side toward enemy

Joe Green

And thank fucking God for
That some of these guys were stoned
All the damn time so then we heard
This noise behind us and then nothing
And then this noise again so I got
Spooked we had these Remington
Full Auto shotguns which you could
Buy on the black market in Saigon
And I just turned around and fucking
Let it go and we heard screams like I never
Heard! That was something big!
"What the fuck was that? " we shouted … deaf
Of course and this guy … what was his name?
The guy who died of sunstroke later
From Arkansas … he went and saw
"It's a fucking tiger, man!" he shouted.
And it was, you know.
I killed a lot of guys in Nam
But I never cried except then."

And these guys go out and
You follow them and they kind of
Slob their way into the car
And you want to say Hey I heard
That fucking story twice already
How many goddamn tigers were there in Nam?
But you saw something.…

Not then. But before … two guys who were
There together one to the other
Trying to remember the name of
Another guy who was killed and

Before that telling their stories …
They made this kind of
Sign to each other which meant
"I'm there, man. I'm there." But trying to
remember there was nothing, trying
To remember the name there was nothing
So this was true. This was true.

The poems that you read
All so typical … the dead soldiers' ghosts
Returning to their girlfriends and wives
Years later and looking on them the silent dead
Looking on "Ladies who were lovely once."

And so in some Greek bar way BC
Two guys drink wine or whatever
And say there is a third guy there
You should have been with us
On the Anabasis those damn Persians
You do an Anabasis you know
When you shout the sea! the sea! it is right.
And who was that guy who got killed in Naxos
You know…?

And really they don't remember
And they slob into their chariot or whatever

And we were in Quang Tri province
Or something like that.
Oh, my.

Uncle Joe

My Uncle Joe O'Brien had a different kind of war.
Didn't go the Basic. Went to the Jersey shore.
How strange life is! But you have to bear and grin it.
When you're a fighting stenotypist who can type 130 words a
  minute!

When the Japs bombed Pearl Harbor Joe was working in DC.
And here's just how it happened as he told it all to me.
The Japs had bombed Pearly Harbor soon all the world would be
  on fire.
Joe thought he'd have a word with old General Strattemeyer.

Who was a major general but in certain quarters passed
As a mellow guy named "Poppy" or, more often, "Straddleass …"
Who put his arm around him. "I just can't help you, Joe
It looks like it's a World war and everybody's gotta go."
Then paused and beamed at Uncle Joe and gave a little laugh.
"Just kidding, Joe I need you. I need you on my staff! "
They gave my Uncle Joe a uniform and all that fiddle dee
Then he and General Strattemeyer went down to Wildwood by
  the Sea
With some other VIPs whose names you'd like to know
But that's a secret history and they're all dead and so
Joe was a stenotypist and a master of the keys
And he went with General Strattemeyer to plan our victories
He was at the Cairo conference and at the Yalta conference too
"Yalta was rather awful but in Cairo—what a view!"
He sat across from FDR. "He was often quite a wreck.
Stalin loved a samovar and so did Chiang Kai-shek
I remember all the words to the song that we once sang

About Stalin and Churchill in a tent with Madame Chiang."
Let's go to '67. And how nothing could really beat a
Drunken happy Uncle Joe singing his version of Aida
With Stalin as the tenor and the soprano Madame Chiang
And the Stone Guest from Don Giovanni requiring them to hang.
"Celeste Aida" is the song that I put on.
When my Uncle Joe was dying back in 2001.
Il tuo bel cielo vorrei ridarti, Le dolci breeze del patrio suol;
Un regal serto sul crin posarti, Ergerti un trono vicino al sol, ah!

Joe Green

Once There Was Childermas Gazelles

Once there was Childermas Gazelles asleep in the green chapel
and food! food! food! and great clipper ships
and President Taft leaning out smiling and smiling into
    symbolic quantities of small arms fire!

There was median and modulus. The promise of parallel
    universes! of a color called panelume!

And we were all magic paradisoadoration jukebox perfection Christmas Titian cortex flung out in the wild blue yonder with a shoeshine and a smile.

The young Goethe plays with his toy theatre!
The Tsar accepts all these restraints with extraordinary serenity
    and moral grandeur!
Jack Ruby gets some good coke!
Henry James writes a letter to his friend!

But now we are void alphabet eggs at best waiting for the spasm war when there will be gulftown galactic lamentation hometowns with bones bones bones and there will be no modulus except deep under Cheyenne mountain where the joint chiefs dream the long dream

Unsyllabled Poontang!

The Ballad of Miss Victoria Minh

I was merry and sad and then sad and merry
When I got off the bus: Downtown Tucumcari.
My friend Hunter had called just two weeks before.
"Come visit me Dooley I'm home from the war!"

He picked me up there and I said "What luck!"
Threw my old army duffle in his Ford Flatbed truck.
I asked "How'd you do it?" He said with a grin
"I guess you remember Miss Victoria Minh."

Miss Victoria Minh she had Saigon eyes:
Thousand yard stare and it was no surprise
That Thomas E. Hunter had Saigon eyes too
Like Victoria Minh's—but his eyes were blue.

"Tell you what, Dooley do you remember that bar?
One of those places you don't want to know where you are."
"Yeah, it was there that you said "Let the Viet Cong win."
Then went into the back with Miss Victoria Minh."

"I thought just the usual whore and we went to the back
But I seemed to have lost my plan of attack.
You think you are dead then something else dies.
I couldn't stop looking at her Saigon eyes."

"You already know, Dooley, it was my second tour"
"Yeah, I already know what are you tellin' me for?"
"I didn't want to go back. But I thought there's something you owe
To all of those guys got killed at Pleih Troeh.

Joe Green

She told me she had a family got killed at Pleiku
Are you listening Dooley? I'm talkin' to you.
You think you are dead then something else dies.
She said she couldn't stop looking at my Saigon eyes."

She said, "You go right now and you have to pay."
She said, "You come see me tomorrow day."
"The next day she gave me a phony passport
And I left Vietnam a hundred days short."

We were merry and sad and then sad and merry
We drove out to the desert outside Tucumcari.
Forgot all about all those usual dooms
Under the stars with those magic mushrooms.

I had my usual visions which consist in the main
Of a convertible Thunderbird in the desert rain.
American roadrunner chasing Wile E. Coyote
I turned to Hunter, said "That's good peyote.

"What are you seeing?" I turned to him.
He said "Peace falling like rain on Victoria Minh."
Then he seemed to have found his plan of attack.
Walked out to the desert and never came back.

You better believe that this is an American song.
I won't admit we did anything wrong.
So put down your glasses once full to the brim
For Thomas E. Hunter and Miss Victoria Minh.

And then have a last drink to Victoria Minh
Who would help a guy out who wouldn't go in.
Have a last drink to Miss Victoria Minh
Who would help a guy out who wouldn't go in.

—*The Loneliest Ranger*

Joe Green

Ronald Reagan Blues

Ronald Reagan got shot in Washington.
Got shot in Washington, D.C.
Ronald Reagan got shot in Washington.
Got shot in Washington, D.C.
They put him in the black car.
He didn't say "Oh, my. Oh, me."

Shot up in the black car
Old Ron made some jokes.
Fucked up in the black car
Old Ron made some jokes.
We'll never know. He'll never know.
We is all just folks.

Tired of the bullshit about him.
Tired of his bullshit too.
Tired of the bullshit about him.
Tired of his bullshit too.
The only thing I really know
Death comin' for me and you.

"Silly motherfuckers," I sd to my friend John.
"Silly motherfuckers. See how they babble on."
John sd "Why you talking to me for anyways?
I got killed in Vietnam."

Luftmensch

The out-of-work painter sketches the ghetto
emptied of its inhabitants,
The painting is filled with objects,
The absence of the living is only temporary
and hints at the most delicious mysteries.
The "somewhat overstocked zoos" of pre-WWII Europe.
Zeppelins are required. Liftships leave every day.
We all took pretty ponies up the golden stairs to the sun.
Extraordinary visions all last night
Along the lake of Silvaplana,
not too far from a certain powerful pyramidal rock near Suler
I was given the envelope.
Into the teacup, quickly, my friends!
The cup (as the mirror shows)
is indeed the cracked yellow one
Otto Frank is now holding in his trembling hands
as the Nazis march down the little street.
But little teacup does make it through!
And the silence and dust are so dear to us.
Later the teacup is filled with the eyelashes of owls.
A wind comes and we waft through the night.

Joe Green

Point Lobos: 1944

In the "heavens" a sword of galaxies burns
Against the hunter's thigh: Orion, that "most tall and
beautiful of men," strides out, a lion's skin on
His shoulders, the star that tips his spear
brilliant lilac and ashy.
His dog is at his heel. He has left a woman.
He is going to find a treasure and
Steps off into space—and falls forever—
Westward across the Pacific; the sword burning,
The speartip brilliant lilac and ashy.
Standing at the edge of the sea,
standing here you would look up and say "Oh, what poetry this
is! What sky-blessed story:"
For this is the poem, the story; the hunter—never mind his
name—Orion, Ulysses, Hercules, his eye on the treasure,
the journey always beginning.
"A journey to find treasure?"
"Oh, the treasure is the journey."
"Orion wanted what?"
"I disremember. But …"
"What?"
"Ulysses only wanted to get home."
"A good story."
I think this story the best our civilization has.
Think of the 600 million dead required to create it.
Let's say Homer started it, though surely it was another peeled Ape of infinite faculties, clubbed to death somewhere in the steppes of Russia. Let's begin with Homer. Four million years to make large animals, perhaps one million years of various modulations of torment to make a Homer.

After the war
They say, his inward eye contracted, he made a poem to draw
The starlight from the thighs of the water. A poem about a restless man. A poem about a liquidation.
Is this a story to
Tell a woman;
A story of killed and killing things, of the gods who
Kill yet live forever? Is this even like nobility?
And … this is the best we have.
I mean this: we will not look at the unhuman heaven.
We live in slave camps and therefore must have our Homer
To sing that the restless man will live forever
As a god.
Perhaps only Jenghiz could tell the truth.
But even he would have his Homer to draw
The starlight from the water
So that
Something human will live forever in the clear dark.
O vile enskyement!
And Homer was the best of the liars
Who made a compact with Death.
What if we saw the actual stars? What
if, for one instant, we could leave behind the vulgarity of our
consciousness and see the unhuman beauty of reality?
But we sicken on what is not even half-real.
Greek civilization goes under.
Another death in the family.
Rome degrades itself. A tortured lip twitches.
"Give me the hammer." Fire dives from the high
air.
A tortured god is not the prettiest of stories. Leave it to the
poets.

"Look at the stars. Orion wants it,
Perseus wants it, even the star-eyed
dog wants it.
But they can't have it—
having been born before Christ flipped a nickel."
Only love can open the sky. There is a
flower in the heart
of the star.
The treasure is the
flower.
We have seen it.
It loves you."
Dante's rose.
What extravagant kindness!
I think that you will find more kindness
in the claws of a lion.
Another thousand years of self-
Importance. The crystal in the granite is a fire wheel.
The Calla Lily is a fire wheel.
Another war and,
in complete candor and acutely aware of the writer's freedom
the public poets thrust Goebbels and Roosevelt
into the sky.
Other poets
(Secure in the goat pasture and looking at the stars)
Speak of art, of religion, of the never-ending story
Of the pure world. Where?
Above
the torture camp?
"You need this," they say. "After the bombings, after
the battle squalor you will need this also." They say, "This is
beauty.

This is love."
It passeth understanding.
They say—the best of them say—
Homer, Dante, Shakespeare say, men at the
extremest limit say,
That this, this hungered emptiness, is beauty.
Therefore:
Civilizations are built on the bones of sleepy children
and this winter, under the Pleiades, there die large numbers.
It is only a trick of deep gravity
that makes the hunter fall westward and graveward to Asia.
All day I listen to the radio.
At night I turn to the nameless stars.
Orion is falling into Asia.
Nothing is falling into Asia.
When will we ever be clean?
Fire.

Joe Green

The Insect Clerks of Neiman Marcus

Lo! The Gods and Goddesses of the new mythology.
The Goddesses are crocodiles in communion dresses!
They wear Adolf of Dachau designer jeans!
They wear necklaces of bird skeletons!
The Gods wear shrouds of petroleum jelly!
They brilliantine their hair.
They turn their mild, Belsen eyes on you
"May I help you sir?" O do not stare!
At secret luncheons they devour larks' hearts.
They devour the intestines of mummys.
They prefer larks three to one.
Three to one.
They have never murdered a baby
Who didn't deserve it.

Listen … Oh! listen!
Hear the twitching of their delicate attennae!
Haie! They come! They come!
Dragging their long
and swelling abdomens!

The insect clerks of Neiman Marcus!
The insect clerks of Neiman Marcus!
The insect clerks of Neiman Marcus!

Beware their dread ovipositors!
Beware their dread ovipositors!
Beware their dread ovipositors!

The insect clerks have come.

There are trapdoors in Cosmetics!
There are trapdoors in Lingerie!
There are trapdoors in Men's Accessories!
There is a secret button in the elevator.

Nightly they descend into vast catacombs.
Buffy! Meagan! Tom! Wesley!
They hang upside down!
They copulate like bats!
They whisper to each other in the languages
Of prehistoric fungi!
And, like Gods everywhere,
They are always hungry.

O Holy Mother!
The store is closing!
They know who you are!
Run! O RUN!

There is a trapdoor in Customer Service.

Down you go
  down
   down
   down
They carry you effortlessly through the tunnels.

They carry you past rooms.
Rooms where small blue clouds weep!
Rooms full of angel guts!
Rooms full of bearded foetuses in bronze caskets.
Rooms where your wife makes love to eels!

Joe Green

(Your wife has a certain eel sex appeal)
Rooms where sores run naked on chandeliers!
Rooms where sewage rats read poetry
In pink peignoirs!

O what is this big room?
It is the Mad Queen's chamber.
It is the throneroom of hearts.
It looks. It looks …
Like the inside of your brain.

The indifferent mandibles let you drop
To the marble floor.

They quietly suck out your eyes.
And then
h! Then!
The Mad Queen comes.
Oh! Oh! Oh! Oh! Oh! Oh!

The dread ovipositor.

You lie paralyzed.

You look out into the "Crevices of Night."

After 80,000 years
Your tears
turn to pearls.

Oh, those were pearls that were his eyes.
Nothing of him but doth suffer....

A Short History

O my ancient father.
My little toy.
My waly water
My little boy.
Wild were my ways
and weird.
Sun blest.
Über alle Gipfeln
Junior.
No rest.
No jaguar
anymore
no mercedes benz
ruh ist die
waly water.
Amen.
Twitch me a new one
baby
let me go down.
Christ's in the old one
honey
lay down.

Francis of the City of St. Francis (for Francis Muir)
Francis of the City of St. Francis
knows that there is
whatever the water wants.

Paddling on the river with Mole.
All these books foolish and beautiful.

Joe Green

One day the Earth says, "Let me guess.
You want it all strange and lovable.

Plateaus
lichen

the Bierstadt moraine

blue herons

Anglo-Saxon farms
the traditions of lovers

John Clare resting his cheek against a stone

a chamberlain of the moon
doves in secret books

rivers
rivers

Finn always Finn again

Dylan Thomas opening the French doors singing

"O Ewigkeit"

guinessess genitive forever

maple

leaves

blown by

a

wind

chasing geese

clouds

seas

and a fire of love from all this

Joe Green

from all this to

her."

"Yes," says Francis.

"No problemo," said the Earth.
And sent this.

"I shall keep in mind my looking in at whatever
it is that is to me you."

At the Hospital

Beside her bed
there is a vase with one flower.
Just before sleep
the flower seems a red-glowing cloud.
When she closes her eyes
the flower inside the cloud awakens.
Conjured by solitude and beauty it opens
as she sleeps.
This flower is a world.
Temples and palaces and
distant villages all in this one flower!
She dreams of a city.
Peach and plum trees shade the roads.
A white jade palace.
Inside the palace
gowns with women bright as green hummingbirds
sing "Celeste Aida."
Their wings hurt.
A slash of ruby at their throats.
They hope that radio will be discovered soon.
They dream that the emperor will love them
nevertheless
The flower beside your bed.
Not impossible.

Joe Green

Dinosaur Love

My friend, who is dying,
was reading *Jurassic Park*
I wanted to shout:
"Why are you reading that?"
You're dying!
You should be reading …
You should be calling …"
"I always liked dinosaurs," he said
and then fell asleep,
one finger between the pages.

Old Father

Baby Belly Butter Little Face
I had a terrible childhood.
I had a problem with Pope Pius XII.
His picture hung in my fourth-grade classroom,
St. Sebastian's Catholic School, Warrensville, Pa, 1958.
I beat him drag racing.
He drove his 600 ft. long gold and white Popemobile
Synchromesh transmission, etc.
I had my bicycle.
And a little luck.
I still remember his face in racing goggles,
the sneer, the Redman tobacco drool at the corner of his mouth.
He called me Kid.
However, there was no doubt who won.
You can't read about it.
The church bought all the newspapers.
The next day nuns descended on sports desks all over the world.
What you can read is: "Pope Beats Smart-Ass Kid."
Don't believe what you read.
They had World Youth day and I wasn't invited.
My father chased me with a belt.
"Why weren't you invited to World Youth Day?"
My mother wept.
Those were terrible days.
The nuns made me write religious poetry.
"The collies/at the funeral home/barked at my grandmother."
Kids fainted nightly from airplane glue.
We lined up to see the movie *The Man With The Atomic Brain*.
My father talked to a cough for twenty years.
We bought Remco telegraph kits

Joe Green

Strung wires from house to house.
Sent secret messages:
"You will be killed in a war."
We all wanted Ted Williams to be our father.
We all wanted our father to take us out and show us the stars,
Hand on shoulder, pipe in hand pointing to a
constellation.
In a field. On a hill.
But our fathers worked for guys who looked like Eisenhower.
They worked the night shift.
They were too tired.
They cried in basements.
They fell one by one into rolling mills.
They left $2500 in insurance.
They were driven to Fairview cemetery by big-knuckled drivers
wearing Masonic rings.
Our mothers were also tired.
Hands caught in mangles at the laundry
They had problems stirring the Kool Aid
They had problems hauling us to church on sleds when it snowed.
You will waste your life.
Someday you will open a book
that will not be the color of the sky.
You will blame the book.
We won't be there.
We will be wailing in coffins.
Wailing for the world to end.
Wailing with all the poor poor dead
For this shitstorm, this storm of shit, to end.
Baby. Belly. Butter. Little Face.
("Whoa," said Little Face. "Hand me down my walking cane!")

Halloween

She's thirteen.
It's Halloween.
"Dad, I'm not going trick or treating this year."
Stunned. Not quite as bad
As when she caught me years ago
Putting the money that the fairy
Left back under her pillow.
"I'm just checking to see if
He left you enough.
That was an important tooth.
Could have been a mixup"

She didn't believe me.

But pretty bad.
"I have a party to go to.
And anyway, I'm too old."
"You're dressing up though?"
"Yeah, I'm going to be an angel."
Thank God.

I offer to make a tin foil halo.
I have a lot of experience at that.
"No thanks, Dad."

But on Halloween
"Hey, the party's at seven.
Want to go—just down the street?"
She does. At six it's dark.
A tiny skeleton down the street.

Joe Green

A perfect moon
A too-cold wind.

I wait as she walks up steps.
Then down the street to a few houses.
White gown, one wing a bit crooked
And anyway too small. Never fly on those wings.

And then the Witch Tree
An old, a twisted oak, bare and bent
Just as is required!

"Remember the Witch Tree?"

"Yeah, we better go."

"Didn't you write a story about it?
A witch who lives under it…?"

"Yeah, we better go."

And she hurries up the street.
Get to the party.

I stay for a second. I have something to say.

Not talking to the monsters everywhere else.

Looking round. Watching her go away.

Getting ready to catch up.

"I'm still here you goddamn witch.

I'm still here."

Joe Green

Just Spring with Chaucer and Some Shriners

Whan in Aprille with its shoures soote,
The Dow declines, the staring Owl sings "Hoota Hoota,"
And I am bathed all in swich liquor:
Johnny Walker Red or sometimes Dewars
Then me lova lova to go um on pilgrimages
And ask a drunken Shriner where his lodge is
And wenden there to myken my complain
Singing nonney nonney hey the wind and rain!
And wanton, dally, smile and jest:
A summer-seeming sprag wit methought the best
That can be doone more than kith and oh! so much less than kind.
Here at the end of an awful century
In the Hungry Mind.
A knycht I am, a parfait gentle wight.
Bodeless my birkin and my pants are tight.
Fell is my feigning and I am rather tired.
My brainpan leaketh and my arms are wired.
Twa corbies natter over my ancient bones.
My leman is lumpish and lubbers low moans.
Ye scenes of childhood! When I ramped
Reckless of the objective world.
My little dust box delicate scamped
My fingers fashed my hair dew curled
My little earth! That one sweet look:
Crying "Abbadabba *die welt zuruck!*"
Erkennt Ihr die Lieder?
My tiny Gluck my *und so weider?*
Oh, I have lost the important connexion to the land.

In a field I am not the absence of the field
And what can I do about it oh Mark Strand?
Ich glaube a clock there was with a sleepy baby face:
A dark veined darling all bedight in lace.
Langsamer war dee day. Komme nicht zuruck.
I saw the movie. I read the book.
The Shriners with their little Harleys,
The thereness, the isness, the beardy bar barley,
The sloppy slop! The happy hop!
Of Aprille when the birdes are braw:
The who shebangadey green green carnival.
And where is Christ with his little pony
And Mary makeless and the winter cherry
The albatross with his abalone
The ant king and the malt fairy?
Therey?
Not very.

Joe Green

IN THE BLUE NOTE

In the Blue Note
you are so sad
your monkey raincoat on.
Your lunchbox with the circus train
gone quite gone again again.
You on wrong side so long.

The snow she no know
Stalin is dead.
Neon throws three roses to the frost.
A mauve cat jumps.
Is lost.
Jumps again.
O Maundy Tuesday! O chalice of rain.
Snowghosts mother the windowpane
Sighing hey down a down.

February! February in the Old Town.
How nice and sad and sad and nice
it is here safe from all harms.
The bargirl's little tits
and when the whisky hits
the nothing you love falling,
falling asleep in your arms.

Chiasmus in Chicago

When the pals of rain come
I know just what to do.
Grab a bottle. Get Old Blue.
Belly crawl across the linoleum
Get under the bunker bed.
Drink till Old Blue is dead.

Then the pals of the pals of rain
and Lamentation Junction
Me want to be sleepy head againe
Another Extreme Unction.
You're a good dog Blue.
And I am too.

Spilling the universe againe
Wild about Harry
The Cubs behind 1 to 10
I will never marry.
Pals, my pals of the pals of rain
I will never marry againe.

Especially not some slushlaced witch
Blabbing upon a peak in Darry
in Californio!
Not unless she's goddamn rich
and I'm drunk againe
and horny O!
and Thelonius is monkerin
and we are sweetly hunkerin

Joe Green

and the rain falls like stones
on our marrowbones.

Trio

At the Starbucks next to
The Barnes and Noble where
Somali cabdrivers huddle in winter
And where last night
I sipped a tall hot chocolate
And read some poetry
The guy with the black overcoat
And the shiny shoes and
The look of what
The look of money looks like
If you are that kind of guy
Asks the poor women across from him
"If you don't mind me asking
How old are you?"
"59," she says the poor woman.
"I have six grandchildren."
"Your time is now," he tells her.
"All the rates go up at sixty."
And she must have told the guy
How much money she had
Because he says "You are in
An excellent position" and tells her
That it might seem ok to have your
Money in the bank with their
So-called guarantee but do we
Really know if the worst happens
Is it really guaranteed and
Six grandchildren that's wonderful
And there are some funds where
She could put her money.

Joe Green

And I am reading that Frank O'Hara poem
"Autobiographia Literari"
That great poem: O'Hara the lonely child
The orphan even birds flew away
From him and then those great last lines
"And here I am, the / center of all beauty!
/ writing these poems! / Imagine!"
And I laugh out loud.
And they both look at me
Like I'm crazy.

Alienation Effect

As that dreadful
Russian, Shklovsky
Has written one must
Make it strange.
Ostranenie!
Viewing it all from a new angle
Like this a poem about
A cat writing a poem
By me, Tippy, a little
Meadow Mouse. So
Here goes! What if I?
No, that won't work
Or I could, ah, that's
So done and done.
I know! As soon as
You finish reading
This poem, me, Tippy,
A little meadow mouse
Right now clinging to
The ledge of the Reichstag
As the Red Army advances
Under me will throw myself
Off this horrible building
Down under the treads
Of a Soviet T-34 tank there
To be squished.
This is the cat
Speaking.

Joe Green

My Left Foot

Doesn't work anymore
One day I got out of bed
And it hurt like hell.
It still hurts.
Even with no weight on it.
And when I stand up
I almost begin to limp.
But not so you can tell.
Things fall apart.
Bodily decrepitude is wisdom.

I'm not ready for this.
But I can almost remember
When "Chookie McCall"
Was not quite an absurd name
For a heroine in a detective novel.
So it's probably polio
Like we used to have
And soon I'll be in an Iron Lung
Yes, soon it will be 1958 again
And all my dead will visit me.
Me in my iron lung.
And eat candy and smoke.
While I look at them
Upside down in the mirror
As they get up and walk away.

The Rain

The rain in 1959 say is
Not the same as the rain in 2005
Which is something a lot of bad novelists forget.
In 1959 it's raining and some kid has
To stay inside or go outside wearing one of those
Yellow raincoats and funny hats
That Dick of Dick and Jane had to wear
And this kid won't do that.
No, he'll watch *Superman*
And George Reeves is still alive
There on the black and white TV
And that 1959 rain is falling
On lilac bushes under which
He once buried a silver dollar
For a whole night and once saw a dead mouse
And the moon that comes out
After the rain when his mother is
In the basement actually ironing clothes
With a mangle and smoking a Lucky Strike
Is a 1959 moon but to get back to
The rain just then a rain was falling on Pusan
And Normandy beach quite different from
The rain for example falling
Today in a suburb here on the coffin
Of some poor kid killed in Iraq
And that kid knew in 1995 at ten
The 1995 rain and now he's dead
And tomorrow it might rain.

Joe Green

OK, THEN ... SO WE'RE IN FREDONIA ...

The corpse on Page 1
Just got up and left
Ok, then ... so we're in Fredonia
Right before the coup.
Down on Moonlight Drive
Near the Palace
And you and me
Are playing chess
It's snowing outside
But we have a nice fire
And there are even sleighs
Whizzing by in the lamplight outside
And we are listening to Ruby Braff.
And suddenly the radio goes off!
They've attacked the radio station!
I said "suddenly the radio goes off!
They've attacked the radio station!'
But the radio keeps on playing.
La la la la la la. And you take my bishop and yawn.
Damn it, when will this poem get started?
And there's a knock on the door!
And it's the corpse on Page 1!
All right!
But he just comes in
And removes the first line.
And the second.
Ok, then ... so we're in Fredonia ...

The Grasshopper and the Ant

My sad friend Ira comes into my office.
"I'm busy Ira."
"I'll just sit here for a while ok?"
Type Type Pretend work.
"Soybean futures are down."
"What?"
"I just lost 4,000 gogooglies."
"So what? You have plenty of gogooglies."
Ira not listening.
Man, I didn't need a sad friend.
Gotta pretend to work and he's there.

Only a sad man
Sad sun setting and in the year 2000
Tells you sitting in the bar after work
Where he has trapped you:

"Never been married.
I am a confirmed bachelor."
Then talks about his 401K
His stocks, the tragedy of loss
And the fact that he still has
467,000 gogooglies invested
In bonds and stocks and
Is movin' on up
In the futures market
And is buying a condo
In the old Northern Pacific offices
The J. J Hill House and Lofts
Robber Baron Bastard

Joe Green

"I don't have a 401K, Ira
No IRA either Ira.
Too confusing and anyway
I hate all that stuff."

Think he'll go away?
No. I interest him strangely.
Slump to my office
"Natural Gas is up.
I didn't buy.
Could have had those gogooglies"

Weekends he is at the library
Reading up on companies.
I'm at the library
Another one
Checking out the *Soul-Life of Plants*
Do they have one?
I would like to know.

Two more winters.
IRA sad but up over 678,000 gogooglies.

Only when, 20 winters from now,
When, shivering in the snow
Old and broke, dragging my old broke ass up
The steps to the J.J. Hill Lofts
Banging on his door.
"Let me in you goddamn ant!"
Will my sad friend be happy.

Which is why.
After all.
I'm here.

Joe Green

The Red Light Is The Blue Light Is

At 16 I hopped a freight
Me dressed as Johnny Yuma
Or maybe Donovan, the little cap
Ok maybe I looked like Dylan
But imagine it. It's dark in Missouri
Down in the railyard and you are
Alone and 16. The freight car is
Yellow in the moonlight and like
A dream. Secrets. No one knows me.
I made it! Where are you going?
Anywhere.
Wish I had done it.
So at 51 I am really on a train,
The Empire Builder!
Coming back from Portland, The Dales,
Spokane, slept through Glacier Park.
No time for ice ages.
Coming back from
Watching my Uncle Joe die.
Drawers and drawers
Of handkerchiefs: a man of
A certain age.
"If you want to
Come," he said. A letter a few weeks
Before "Cancer. Oh, well … it sure
Was fun smoking all those Chesterfields.
Oh, well. I'm saving all the newspapers
To wrap the china."
And the train stops.
As trains do in the dark.

No reason that you know.
Now look at the schedule:
Wolf Point MT. Yes.
Look out. Hourless Prairie.
The moon's moon is in the sky!
Maybe someone's Uncle has died.
Maybe the engineer needs a smoke.
Maybe ghosts loading buffalo skins.
Moving again and past the town.
All these towns built on the
Bones of sleepy children.
Stops again. Same moon. More ghosts.
Moving toward Minot:
Spooky for sure.
No place for Joe, of course
Then coming up to Williston.
Jorgensen's Roughrider Liquor!
Train stops for ten minutes.
Think I can make it?
No.
Next train 23 hours and
About 45 minutes from now.
15 dollars in my pocket.
Took the wrong credit card.
Standing on the platform
Suitcase on the train.
The red light is.
The blue light is.
Wish I could tell Joe.
Oh, well.

Joe Green

Incident on Fifty-second Street

"I sit in one of the dives
On Fifty-second Street
Uncertain and afraid."

It was Christmas Eve 1939.
W.H. Auden was waiting for a sign.
"Been to China, been to Spain.
Lord, lord don't want to do it again.
The Christmas star rages with its usual vengeance.
Lord, lord give me a little transcendence."

Lord, lord that's what he prayed
At the end of a low, dishonest decade.
Drinking alone. Then who comes in?
My Uncle Joe. Auden buys him a gin.
They fall in love. There is a back room!
Boom a lay Boom a lay Boom a lay Boom!
They went back to the bar and unless I miss my dates.
Auden wrote "In Memory of W.B. Yeats."
Showed it to Joe who kept on drinking.
"I like this place" is what he was thinking.

Coatesville 1

Driving into Coatesville past Our Lady Queen of Peace
My old friend Tommy says "We still got that at least."
Fifty-six years old. Years of junk and speed and crack.
Tommy says, "Dooley, you know sometimes
I think I'm not coming back."
Pulled into Gaby's. Drank and talked till way past dark.
Tommy says, "Jesus didn't die alone. You can read it in Luke or
 Mark
But sometimes I can't hardly breathe I feel so alone."
I say, "Tommy, I got to leave." Roll back stone.

Coatesville 2

"It's a hard world," my dad says.
"It's a hard world and you can't win.
You're always going out
Even when you think you're going in.
It's a hard world. It's a hard world, Dooley."
I know, Dad. I know it truly.
91 years old. Can't see. Can't hear. Can hardly talk.
Dad says, "You got to leave. Pick up yourself and walk."

Joe Green

Last Night

Last night I was watching *Panic in Needle Park*
1971 with Al Pacino playing a junkie
And what's her name? Kitty Winn … playing his girlfriend
A sweet girl but then, inevitably, a junkie and then a whore.
He betrays her and then she turns him in when she gets in
        trouble.
Nothing personal really and when he gets out of jail
And sees her … a perfect ending. He says "You comin?"
Junkies in New York. I knew this one and that one.
All dead now and I remember John calling me
"I have bad news we lost Kevin." "Lost?"
This one and that one and I would remember if I could.
But instead I feel desperate for 1971 to see what's left
What will be left which is a certain slur of colors
There out on the streets and this is what will be left:
The movie. Need a dime to make a call. Yes.
The VW the narcs drive now looking so strange.
But at the end a slur of color. And I am grateful even for this.

Today my father is dying. Went in won't come out.
"Failure to thrive" Which means he won't eat. Doesn't want to eat.
Just two weeks ago not all there then he still
Asked me if I could go home and get his razor.
The good one. And pointed at the tree outside his window.
And said something. But now my brother says even
That whatever is gone him gone except for the part
That worries about how he's going to pay for all this.
Which I am grateful for. I remember the old lady
in the Williams poem on her last ride seeing trees
A blur asking "What are those?" "Trees"

"I'm tired of them too." So much is left behind.

Which is the easy thing to say but not right.
Or at least you know that this one and that one
Is gone and there was a certain look.
Tired then I remember of the bullshit of, for example, war
And then tired of the bullshit about the bullshit of war
And then not even tired or now so what but
I would remember if I could. I'd remember my father if I could.
2 AM stomach pains. He called my brother to take him.
Chinese doctor in the emergency room and my father asks
"Are you Jewish?" The doctor laughs. And my father says.
"Why are you laughing? It's not funny. I need a professional here."

Joe Green

A Very Fine Fiddle Had She

When my mother was four
She got out of her bed
To see off the soldiers
At least that's what she said.
She walked five miles from the farm
And stepped on a nail
But it did little harm
She was swept up in a gale
That carried her straight to
A green field in France
Where she wasn't too late
To see the white poppies dance
"I thought it was pretty"
She said to me.
"Now, let me tell you
Of the 'Fiddler of Dee'"

My Demented Mother

Took my mother to see my father.
It was my brother's plan.
"Tell me, Jim, oh tell me
Who was that old man?"
His death it wasn't easy.
We followed him through the town.
"This place looks pretty sleazy
Can't we drive around?"
Drove on past the movies.
Or at least where they had been.
"We snuck into the movies
Walking backwards going in."
West Grove cemetery.
"Do you know where you are?"
"Damn it, Joe, of course I know
And I'm staying in the car."
I don't want to see. I don't want to see.
The breaking of the bough.
When her mother died my wife turned to me.
"I am an orphan now."

Joe Green

After Twitter

Let us go then you and I.
No, we cannot be bitter.
To our new home in the sky
And we will not remember Twitter.

We will go and bid the soldiers shoot
To get with child a Mandrake root
Then stagger to the Mermaid Tavern
Avoid the pit, eschew the cavern
And there cry out just what we know
Tales of weakness, tales of woe.
Then sip our ale and wait for one
William Blake? Maybe John Donne!
For God's sake given where we were
I'd take Walter De La Mare
No one comes. We wait an hour.
The off we go to the Dark Tower.
From the Mermaid to the bower.
Ben asks to wait another hour.
We'll wait an hour more at least.
"Ah, look Ben—what rough beast!"
Slouching out from Bethlehem
To say "Hello!" to me and Ben
Face of Auden. Eyes of Yeats.
Custom built to serve, it waits.
Chats a bit … says it was built in
A railway town by the name of Milton.
Asks the way to Simplon Pass
Says that it must go, alas
Can't find the way. It's lost you see

In Seven Types of Ambiguity.
And we are lost but long for that …
And Macavity the Mystery cat
Is there and then, ah then
We meet the long world's gentleman.

A few years ago my dad was dying
I sat beside him trying trying
To be anywhere but there
To be anywhere no where.
Held his hand as I read a book.
Didn't really want to look.
The Resistance. Nazis in the mist.
Felt him shake and then I kissed
Him … when was the last time I…?
I looked at him. I watched him die.
Then he whispered, "I need you …
There's one thing I want you to do.…"
Then I couldn't hear just what he said.
I went away then he was dead.
See the granite on his tombstone glitter.
Then we're gone too. Twitter. Twitter.

Joe Green

OLD POET   YELLOWKNIFE

Once Jung and Freud were arguing
And you can read about it
Like I did today
And Freud pissed his pants
And Jung offered to psychoanalyze him
Years later Freud was rolling into
Some town where Jung lived
And decided not to drop by
Can you blame him?
But this is called
In psychoanalytic circles the
"Kreutzenhollerin Blick"
Or something like that.

When Jung was a baby
He had two personalities
Number 1 and Number 2
But that's ok ... so did his mama
Years later he was asked to come back to Germany
Declare Hitler insane
He preferred not. He was busy.
"And who isn't crazy these days?"

Crazy men is leading us, my friends

Even before my First Communion
I knew I had to get away.
School? Nuns?
A town with a West End and an East End?
Who signed me up for this?

You don't get no points in
Those louche joosh joints.

Runnin' from the Paterrollers.

Shortcut through Fairview cemetery
Goin' to the library
With a note from my mama.
"Please let Dooley take out any book he wants"
Knew all about zombies
So when my grandmother got up from the grave
And followed me down
The weasel around her neck with its red eyes
Her sayin' "The turkey is a little dry, Jean."
I didn't say "Feets don't fail me now."
Might have whistled a bit though.

The Patterrollers.

And when oh them cigarette girls got up
Dead after 30 years at Sun Ray Drugs
Following me down and when all them
Patterrollers started following me
Maybe I walked a little faster
Quick look behind but
They was circlin' round.

"Who isn't crazy these days?"

And then at the library.
"You can't take out that book."
That note from your mama

Joe Green

Doesn't cut any ice."
I stole the book.

Outside all my Zombies.
Bowing before me.
Crying "Ourance. Ourance!"

Which wasn't my name.

And is the point.

It's ZERO degrees here in Yellowknife
And we is grateful.

I am in my little room
And when death comes
We gonna have a "Kreutzenhollerin Blick"
Death on the street. I lean out the window.
Like Scrooge on Christmas Day!
"We're havin' a "Kreutzenhollerin Blick," Mr. Death.
And I am not at home to you."
Him goin away saying
"Who isn't crazy these days?"
And I won't answer the door either.
That's how they got Mozart.
I'm waitin' for the Groovemaster.

—*The Loneliest Ranger*

WHAT IS POETRY?

Here in Yellowknife
At the Artificial Limb and Brace
We got a lot of "Nature."
Never liked Nature much though.
"He died. Oh, well, it's a natural thing."
So what I don't understand is
Why anyone would like it.
"If your grandmother ain't in heaven
Why are you thinking about her?"
Well, we tried.

Here we got the Aurora Borealis
And people who say
"He looked like a moose in the headlights."
Over and over.
Just like the old aurora.
But what do they want?
I don't worry about it.

After all I ain't natural
An old man stuck all the way here
Playing his banjo singing "Sweet Lorraine"
Dreaming of a white snake with soft brown eyes
Like Nature never thought of
Polar snake, all white fur,
A sweet little guy you could talk to.
Named "Lorraine."

"All Nature is a Heraclitean fire
Pray you, avoid it."

Joe Green

We got a lot of one-armed Inuit
Since the introduction of the
Snowblower by the White Man.

It's why I'm here, baby.

—*The Loneliest Ranger*

Trout Fishin' in Yellowknife

Up here in Yellowknife
We don't worry about the wars
Against Aesthetic Idealism or whatever.
The war is there but we don't go to it anymore.
(Thank you Mr. Hemingway.)

We worry about our little dogs.

"Hoppy, I'll let you out but don't
Go down to the Borealis fields!"
But he does anyway and it's so cold there.
Brings back what's froze.
Our Iniut calls them the "Breath of the Stars."
Always so romantic.
They want it all so strange and beautiful.

Old radio shows frozen.
The Third Man. I loved that.
Could have done without
The Great Guildersleeve though.
And those last words ... all tangled up in Hoppy's fur.
They thaw and then you hear them.
"Help." "Mommy" "Ah, fuck" "No, no, no."

Heard Goethe's the other night.
No, he didn't say "More light! More Light!"
Hoppy just standing there.
Wants to go out again.

Joe Green

"Ok, Hoppy, you tell me.
When did Poetry ever change a thing?"

Wants to go out.

"Arf," he says.

"Arf. Arf. Arf."

—*The Loneliest Ranger*

A Catholic Negro in Pittsburgh

The existence of that spiritual entity
AKA "The Groovemaster"
Is proven by St. Thomas Aquinas.
As you would know
If you stepped in like me
Into a pawnshop in Pittsburgh, Pennsylvania
Which is right near "The Poor People Banque"
Past the old guy telling another old guy
"I tell you what. There ain't no hustlers like us anymore."
Just like what I bet Jesus said really
Goin' to take a look at the tambourine
And you see that 45 record
Shining there from the Groovemaster.

And you remember you is safe
Like when in "The Exorcist" they listen
To the devil talking and say
"It's English—but backward. What an asshole."
Which starts everything right up
The calling of the exorcist, the young priest
Saying "Take me" and going to heaven
The little girl not remembering anything then

Not remembering—what you hope for the poor whores
Shivering there as you leave
You thinking of that Groovemaster song.

Joe Green

Safe. We are safe. We just don't know it.
The Groovemaster coming at the end of days.

—*The Loneliest Ranger*

The Tale of the Tinker Transported

I was born beneath the thistle bush.
I leapt up from the clay!
My heart sang like a dying thrush
His young love far away.

I was born in the wildwood drear
But there I could not stay.
Though Jesus be a grenadier
And I a clock of clay.

I went to be a soldier man.
But there I could not stay.
Dying by some stranger's hand
In lands so far away.

Then I would a sailor be.
But there I could not stay.
There were many famous victories
But I was far away.

I stayed then with a Gypsy girl
All winter in a valley.
She had black eyes and raven curls
And I called her Dirty Sally.

When summer came I left her there
In the gypsy caravan, oh!
And stepped out smart to take the air
Of the wide and wakening land.

Joe Green

I was learning the tinker's art
And walked on through the Fall
And mended many a maiden's heart
With my long peggin' awl.

Oh, stamen stiff and pistil sweet
All on the livelong day!
He that would temptation meet
Is but a clock of clay.

And then I met a demure lass.
It was in Dublin city.
She would sit and watch the fine folks pass
All evening by the Liffy.

I am but a country lad
But many a maiden have I seen, oh..
But none with eyes so bright and mad
And none with eyes so green.

"I am a merry tinker lad
My young love," I did call.
"I've got a thing to mend," she said.
"If you have brought your awl."

Oh stamen stiff and pistil sweet
All on a winter's day.
He that would temptation meet
Is but a clock of clay.

So she sang like the cuckoo.
I sang like the thrush.

There were two birds in the garden
And one bird in the bush.

"Now then," said the fair maid
"Will you marry me?
And carry me far far away
Across the wine dark sea?

My father is a Captain grim
Many stories I could tell, oh!
He likes his whores and he like his gin
And my life's a living hell."

"Oh, hush now lass and do not cry
Of this you'll have no doubt
I'll take you to Australia
If you'll blow the candle out."

And we beguiled the wild wild night
And the wild wild wind did blow.
I left her in the cold daylight
Before the cock did crow.

So it's farewell bonny lassie
I'll never married be
Though I become a vicar
And have Jesus Christ to tea.

Then I put on my tinker's pants
And my tinker's coat
And kissed her oh so softly
And took a half-pound note.

Joe Green

So, it's farewell bonnie lassie
I'll never married be.
Though Jesus be a sailor
And love the pure whiskey.

So out I slipped into the hall
But who do you think I see?
The Captain grim with a quart of gin
And a pistol on his knee.

Oh, stamen stiff and pistil sweet
All on a winter's day.
He that would temptation meet
Is but a clock of clay.

I woke up in six iron bands
The captain said "I'll tell ya
You're going to Van Diemen's land
Near far away Australia."

Now I make do with lizard stew
And heed the wombat's call
And mend the hearts of kangaroos
With my long peggin' awl.

Kwanzaa Christmas Tango

If you're rich, then everything's easy
You just take a jaunt to Belize
And sit on the beach and dare eat that peach
And you hardly ever feel queasy.

If you're poor, you ain't in no trouble
If there is a stock market bubble
You fell quite rested with nothin' invested
And when it breaks you get nothin' in double.

But what can you do if you is a Christmas tree Jew
And it's the third night of Kwanzaa
And you're black and Catholic and Argentinean too?
You just sing like Mario Lanza

"O Sole mio
I love Dolores Del Rio
But my sheikhy dashiki's on fire
And Bacall was so hot
In *To Have and Have Not*
And if you say not you're a liar."

And you is alone as you is writin' this poem
Alas for the Jeunesse Dorée
You is alone. Alone in your home
And there's only one thing you can say:

"O Sole mio
I love Dolores Del Rio
But my sheikhy dashiki's on fire

Joe Green

And Bacall was so hot
In *To Have and Have Not*
And if you say not you're a liar."

Night of the Hunter

"Let's go, please" my poem said.
"C'mon."
"You sure you're not too old
for the Merry-Go-Round?" I asked

But I loved it and she knew.
And so we went and I watched her.
I should have known then:
The solemn look on her face as she rode.
It was the last time.
I watched it whirl … there she was … and there.

And now and then the white elephant.

Gone for a year and Halloween.
I thought I would see her tonight.
Running in the dark TOWARD me.
The porch light is on.
No one came.

And then I read about her!
She had changed her name to Delia
Lived with Mingus Colorados
And she played a fair Ophelia
In a forlorn summer playhouse
In some godforsaken town.
"Dooley, I think I can do Neil Simon
Now that I've got Shakespeare down."

Delia's gone. Oh, Delia's gone.

A postcard.

"Dooley, Sourdough mountain is sooo beautiful.
There are seven or nine stars in the Pleiades!
I'm learning to play the autoharp!
Gary Snyder says to say Hi!"

A phone call.

"Where?"
"New York, Dooley! I'm having dinner
At Sardis!
I know where the ducks go—just like Holden
I'm in love!
Do you know Frank O'Hara?"

Alone then for years
I saw the pictures and she looked the same:
The photogs with their Speed Graphic cameras
The men beside her.

Alone and then a call.
"I'm sorry. I'm downstairs can I please come up?"
"Yes!"

And she was there!
Older. I liked her hair
It must have been raining
And she
Was sobbing "Oh, the others … I didn't …

I mean …"

And I looked at her … all she put me through
… all the others and we still had a chance
One good line. One good line!

And I looked at her
Afraid to touch her.

"Baby," I said. "You don't have to
say anything.

Baby, I don't care!"

That was years ago.
And I am alone.
Now I can only write on trains.
Like the guy who wrote
Night of the Hunter
One fist said "Love"
The other said "Hate."
"It's not dark yet …"

Yeah, I know.

Joe Green

That

That real bed and that real room
Are as real as that unreal tomb
You will never see. All unreal.
Life then Death and what you feel
Is what is always really real.
I knew a man who could have lived, but then
He shot himself and I remember when
His brother told me he, himself, felt dead.
"He killed us," is what his brother said.
Finished his drink and then went home to bed.

The archduke rose and smiled and left
The usual suspects felt bereft
And walked into the general snow
Wondering why he had to go.
The cats remained right near his chair
And didn't really seem to care
But that is simply feline seeming
They sat and dreamed and kept on dreaming
Of something we can never know
Bereft and left in the general snow.

My Mojo All Gone

My mojo all gone I wish I were Ashbery
No, not the poet. I'd have a haberdashery
Ashbery's Haberdashery down thirteen flights.
We're closed all the days and all of the nights.
We'd have derbies and Panamas and the finest fedora
And a curious headdress from far Bora Bora
And a nautical hat that's most like a whale
And none of it, sadly, quite yet for sale.
Cause that's just what happens. That's how it goes.
Without rings and your fingers or bells on your toes
You close up the shop and go down to the zoo
And patiently stare at a panther or two.
As they patiently stare right back at you

My mojo all gone so I cry out thinly
I want to write poems like Phyllis McGinley.
If luck were a lady I'd be in Manhattan
And there'd be a *New Yorker* to put this and that in.
I'd have an apartment quite near the West Side
And a small quaint log cabin quite near Telluride.
And on weekday mornings I'd write poems of wit.
Then repair to the bedroom and sleep for a bit.
The slow snow would fall but I'd still go to Macy's
And then on up to Harlem to listen to Basie.
I'd understand Swing but be the upset by the Blues.
Have a fine fox-fur coat and fine two-tone shoes.

Joe Green

The Cats of Paree

It's been many years since I've been to Paree
Where I played for that French girl. Her name was Marie.
And she sang, she sang so lyrically.

"*Oui*, I'm a cat."
"I don't care about that.
But don't you think you could play in B-flat?"

I murmured "*Oui*" as I changed the key
And Marie she sang so beautifully.
A beautiful song without any "*Rien*"
And when it was over she sang it again.

I'd felt half dead. This was in '45.
But as Marie sang I felt quite alive.
Ah, that beautiful song without any "*Rien*"
Just me and Marie. That's the way we were then.

All over. All over. Yet what can I say?
Well met by moonlight on the Champs-Élysées!

The words of my daddy I still can recall
"If you just write light verse then you're nothing at all."
This was in the Fifties and there were many sad men
Who remembered their twenties in the Forties and then
Wrote many sad poems where they danced the tango
With sweet girls from Paris "It was long ago
In Forty-five after the Germans had gone
She was so sweet and so pale and so wan

She was so sad and when we went to bed
"Just hold me, please hold me," was all that she said.
And the room was so cold and there was no light
And the cats of Paree howled all the damn night."

Joe Green

Ship Poem

We did Donne when Donne was done.
This was back in '71.
When we were done with Donne
Then we did Herbert
And Vaughn and Traherne before sherbet.
And those who were inclined to Pope.
Were very much inclined to dope.
And those who declined to Wallace Stevens
Were left alone. We had our reasons.
You is young and you think you're wise.
Then your museum burns down and your elephant dies.
Many years have passed and it isn't far
Through Villion, Nashe and then Dunbar.
You is gettin' old and you think you're wise.
Then your museum burns down and your elephant dies.
More years have passed and now I see
I'm very much inclined to me
In my little boat on the wine-dark sea.
You is old and you think you're wise.
Then your museum burns down and your elephant dies.

Christopher Smart

Christopher Smart
Was lucky that
He wrote a fine poem
About a fine cat
If you read the poem
I think you will agree
That the poem's damn fine
And so is Jeoffry
Good old Kit Smart
Wasn't particularly sad
That just about everyone
Thought he was mad
When he would fall on his knees
To pray in the street
They would all creep away
On their little feet.
But poor old Kit Smart
He had one big fan
"I'd as lief pray with Kit Smart
As with any man."
Said Doctor Johnson
And then he went out
To drink lots of coffee
And complain of his gout
Yes, Doctor Johnson
Had much common sense
Though he knew not the wherefore,
the why or the whence
"Thus I refute, I refute
Bishop Berkeley."

Joe Green

He pounded the table
And did it right smartly
Things seemed to him
Just how they appear
A miniature sleigh
And eight tiny reindeer
Hardly, if ever,
Appeared to his vision
And if they once did
He'd made a decision.
"Thus I refute, I refute
Bishop Berkeley."
He pounded the table
And felt rather sparkly.
While Christopher Smart
Who had cats in his belfry
Wrote "Jubilate"
With his fine cat, Jeoffry.

Tiny Tim Blues

Went up to Minnesota.
Took my little uke.
Went up to Minnesota.
Took my little uke.
They called me Tiny Tim.
But I felt just like a fine young Duke.

Went on Johnny Carson.
Married a fine young gal.
Said "Hi" to Johnny.
Johnny was my pal.
All over. All over.
Knew it would be anyhow.

When you think about it,
You know they all knew my name.
When you think about it,
You know they all knew my name.
Who knows you my friend, my friend?
But at the end we're all the same.
All the same.

Lying in my grave.
Minnesota snow blow wild.
Lying underground.
I feel just like a little child.
Come the end times, the end times, the end times
Eternity feel so mild.

Joe Green

You Are a Star

The Buddha is a baby
in the baby Buddha palace.
You are a star.
You never heard of him.

The baby Buddha
smiles at the peacocks.
You are a wisp of cloud.
Just then you are snoozing.

Little Buddha points at the moon
pale crescent shining.
You are a coin
buried in deep grass.

Spring rain.
Buddha iris in the golden chapel.
You are born.
You love your little life.

The Buddha is a baby
in the baby Buddha palace.
You are a star.
You never heard of him.

Arrayed for the Bridal

Arrayed for the bridal she looks so nervous
Her mother beside her she didn't want to go in.
She cried all last night imploring the service
Of all of the angels on the head of the pin.

"Oh, take me away to a small town out west
Where I'd work as a waitress in a broke down cafe
And live right above it. That would be best.
And work some nights and only part if the day.

And maybe I'll write him a letter sometime
And have a cowboy send it for me.
"I got a small room and I'm feeling quite fine
In fact I'm feeling quite free.

I have a small bed, one table and chair
The Gypsy Girl hangs on the wall
And as for the rest why you know it's not there
I have a few things and that's all.

But I have that old book you once gave me, Joe
The Rag and Bone Shop of the Heart
And read it sometimes just so I will know
To be true we must be apart."

But none of the angels heard a damn word.
They laughed and laughed in their dancing.
For she was a Methodist and the thought is absurd
That they would stop, for an instant, their dancing.

Joe Green

And so she was married on an old winter's day
Perhaps it was all for the best.
But sometimes she dreams as the old records play
Of that broke-down café way out west.

No More A-Roving

NOTHING made Wordsworth sad.
Old Sam Coleridge thought "Too bad."
They kept on writing—not for spite
But to apprehend the endless night.
And because that is what they did
They even somewhat liked that kid:
John Keats was the poor boy's name
Who couldn't stand the endless same
And one day, well, he just took off
To Rome because he knew his cough
Meant that soon he would be dead.
"Oh, my poor friend" is what he said
To his friend who watched the poor guy die.
And Keats still wondered "Who am I?"
And knew he would be nothing soon.
The endless night. The falling moon.

Joe Green

Dreamland

It is a nice nursing home.
And it has a fine smoking lounge
Where you can be completely alone
And listen to "Sweet Georgia Brown."

Invisible hand. Invisible band.
You is old and think of your mother.
But the band plays as it's going away
In smoke. So why should you bother?

There was this and then there was that.
You should have got out of that town.
But you is just where you is at.
They go up and then they go down.

Some Last Words

Someone called *"Der Alte Professor."*
The little man behind the curtain.
"I am OZ the great."
Toto knows but is nice to him.
He is so nice to him.
He loves the little guy.
Later, they all step inside a tangerine
and ride pretty ponies up the golden steps
to the sun.
The sun says, "Go home and go to bed."
So they do: lion, scarecrow, tin man,
Dorothy, Toto, Old Professor.
They dream of a carousel in a park in winter.
They dream of the snow that seems so shy.
The delicate mouth of the giraffe.
The white elephant.
This mirror shows them sleeping.
Why do they seem so forsaken?

Joe Green

Canarios or The Escape of D.B. Cooper

As when, oh, as when
Any small shining clock arrives.
A beautiful odd-shaped boat prepares for love.
Our children's bluish car his little caw thinking
Sees her golden round fancy clock laugh.
A silver sport shoe is on fire.
Yet the bluish gun abides.
Mine silver well-crafted book fidgeting thinks.
As when any little cat smiles and an expensive mouse walks.
Our shining picture runs as soon as his round soft house walks.
The stupid soft gods get an idea as soon as her daughter's
expensive mouse looks around while the fancy magazine fails
and her daughter's white camera got an idea too.
The red car sleeps or a given little tall picture is.
Any given silver camera fidgeting.
Our children round guns walk.
Our children whose white white silver
moon smiles as soon as his tall odd sha!
As when the purple exam book falls.
A given red adheres or maybe their tall expensive purple golden
    green tall clock falls.
Mine smart glove walks at the place where our children's
    beautiful balloon snores
Whose sloppy love shows its value and perhaps our children's red
    sloppy caw of a crowcar snores.
The smart expensive bicycle snores.
Any green magazine looks around while a well-crafted spoon of
    the color panelume snoozes
His brother's smart white mobile phone calms-down however,
the silver tall door stares or any beautiful forge lies.

As when a round white angel sings
And any silver omprella is angry.
Any round small stupid camera stares the time that mine green
 eraser fidgeting so nervous rests.
A sloppy exam book stands-still while a round-shaped door
 stands-still
or maybe her daughter's white phone calculates and still any
golden golden golden lostlove calms down and her daughter's
 green wine calms down
while
her
daughter's
golden
ram
arrives as when if only the cat comes home and he does!
D. B. Cooper jumps from that plane
To oh! what strange stars and skies
Where the clock never ticks or tocks
Under the sign of the constellation
Vulpecula!
The blue fox.

Joe Green

Vaudeville

Vaudeville transcends all love
You have a hat and just one glove
And perhaps a cane. It is enough!
You know we are the stuff
Dreams are made on. As was said
By some guy who finally went to bed
After all the shows and shows.
What vaudeville means … why, no one knows.

Love is love and love is nil
Without the thrill of vaudeville
When love is there why love has flown
And you discover you must dance alone
Not for yourself. Ah, that's the key
And is vaudeville's great mystery
You look out always from the stage
And hear the music and feel the rage
Of dancing always against death.
There! And this. You take a breath
And put out one foot and then another
Never wondering why you bother
You dance for you. You dance for her.
You dance and it does not occur
That as you dance you name your love
Or think of the paper moon above.
You dance to live and love just then.
To conquer where. To conquer when.
And because not to do that would soon kill
The human love that's vaudeville.

Third Murderer

I saw Warren Buffet on a tuffet.
He kicked my ass.
I showed Donald Trump my Heffalump.
He turned on the gas.

It's hard out here. You can't hardly gets your breath.
With all these Third Murderers. Like in Macbeth.

Tom McGrath is dead.
And Adorno is too.
Many more have fled.
This overstocked zoo.

It's hard out here. You can't hardly gets your breath.
With all these Third Murderers. Like in *Macbeth*.

Poetry doesn't change a thing.
You're not sure that's right.
You awake and sing
The World of Lite.

It's hard out here. You can't hardly gets your breath.
With all these Third Murderers. Like in *Macbeth*.

Everything's ok.
You got your Sunday toot.
All's a play.
Go, bid the soldiers shoot.

Joe Green

It's hard out here. You can't hardly gets your breath.
With all these Third Murderers. Like in *Macbeth*.

Angels is coming.
Trumpets are flourishing.
He knows were dumb
And continually perishing.

It's hard out here. You can't hardly gets your breath.
All my pretty ones? All? Just like in *Macbeth*.

Poem Written at Twenty Below

Up here in Yellowknife we got a weekly paper.
Comes out once a month.
"First baby of 2005 born to the Olsens!"
Of course.
You can't go by Pat's Czech American Grill without wanting to
    go in."
So true.
Got a guy who writes a column: "From My Fiery Heart."
Really. One of those "did you ever?" things.
"Did you ever notice the sound the snow makes
When it's falling and it's 20 below?"
Can't say what it is. But it's a serious sound.
That's serious snow.
Got another guy … the one who wrote the poem
About the snowplow driver in Chicago in '71
Who went crazy—plowed fifty-four cars into the river.
The poem was "oddly sympathetic to the driver" they said.
Icicles on Bicycles.
Our town is "Our Town"
Rescuing Polacks from snowdrifts happens most days.
On the hill the cemetery
And the dead talking.
Married six years and she's on the hill and …
Someplace in my house I have a letter
From my great-aunt.
Her boy, Noel, missing in North Africa, 1942.
Missing not dead she said
Missing not dead she said and ten years later
I have the letter she wrote
"Oh, who will help me find my baby boy?"

Joe Green

There's the Little Indian Sioux River off the Echo trail.
Really.
You say everything twice when it's twenty below.
Except:
When the planet was young sailing ships conducted
commerce upon the five mighty oceans of Barsoom,
traveling from one fabulous port to another.
Which is what works for me
At twenty below.

The Tall Hair Blues

They say I'm ugly and they're right I guess.
They say I'm ugly and they're right I guess.
Some say I look like a plugged up Porgy.
Some say I look like a drunked up Bess.

Went down to the Mojo Man asked him what I can do.
Went down to the Mojo asked him what I can do.
Told him I want some of that sweet sweet loving too.

He said "Drink this potion. Then get outta my place.
Drink up this motion potion and get outta my place.
Give me fifty dollars. I don't want to see your face.

You'll look like a Beatle. That potion make your hair grow long.
Maybe you'll look like Ringo. But your hair gonna be long.
Maybe you got an ugly hairstyle. Maybe that's all that's wrong."

But I ain't like the others. Hair roll and flow so beautifully.
But I ain't like all the others. Hair roll and flow so beautifully.
I'm the Lonliest Ranger. My poor hair grow vertically!

Went down to South Philly. Gals give me such looks!
Went walking down South street. All the gals give me those looks.
One said "Hey mister, you in those record books?"

Walked away from those mean women. Hair got caught up on a
    electric wire.
Walked away from those mean women. Wire was twenty feet or
    higher.
Listen to em all. "That funny man's on fire."

Joe Green

When you got tall hair you're gonna ride the Midnight train.
When you got tall hair you're gonna ride the Midnight train.
Have to sit on top of the coal car. Smokestack lightning in your brain.

The Tall Hair Blues.

To Tim Smith

How old was I when we first met?
Thirty something? I forget.
You were working for the army
And we were both so very barmy
You laughed as you typed and we knew
… About the bridge at Elkhorn slough
And about the owl in the Owl Oak
And Samson Shillitoe, that bloke.
And Connie knew and laughed with us
So I flew here just to discuss
Just when in fact that she would assent
To be with me together blent
So there was a method to our madness
Song and poem and what gladness
That I take it for a rainbow sign
As we begin our slow decline
Or just maybe that has passed
And we descend ah fast ah fast
Where all, of course, come to the end.
Heigh ho for the carrion crow, my friend!
Which, of course, I don't really mean
Who the hell knows …
Your friend,

Joe Green

Joe Green

Rejoined with:

Timothy L. Smith

Those were the days, me lad,
more merry than sad
and nobody could assail us!
Now the world's gone awry
and though we may try
… we must admit that things fail us.

No more can I stand with a jug in my hand
and declaim many poems from memory.
And where once I was rich, and a sonofabitch
now I'm just an old asshole in penury.

Oh the passing of days has its myriad ways
of cutting us all down to size.
But I say, "What the fuck, I've still had good luck
and I'll never give in to Time's lies.

As the man said, "So it goes" and nobody knows
what waits as the golden years call.
As for you and for me, we'll just have to see
if we can't beat the odds after all.

Outta Here

I wait beneath the willow.
So many young people.
The young men with their young women dancing.
Fireflies and a moon above.
Screw them all.
Lawn party ... why am I here?
I need another martini.
I would go but my wife took my keys.

The Stars The Stars

All the night the moon shone
The stars burned in the golden sky,
I watch *Gilligan's Island*
On an old black-and-white TV.
I pass the window to get another drink
Thinking of the Professor.
There is no other life.

Joe Green

All the Holy Night

The immensity of the universe!
Reading the *New Yorker*
A nice *New Yorker* cartoon.
Skipping the shitty poems.
My martini is so cold.
Look there's a cartoon I missed!

Something to Count On

The moon is like a gypsy playing a yellow guitar.
A martini is just a martini.
Every damn time.

The Plum Wine of the Buddha

The Plum Wine of the Buddha
Cannot properly be called a cocktail.

In Martini Veritas

After five martinis
Soft jazz
Still sounds like shit.

Night, Fog, War

"You, sir, are no gentleman,"
My poem said.
I lit two cigarettes
One for me, one for him.
Two on a match.

"Just like the movies,"
he said.

"Well, she's gone," I said.

Night. Fog. War.

"Of all the gin joints
in all the towns in all the world,
you had …"

"Shut up," my poem requested.

"Let's just go."

Introduction to the Rin Tin Tin Poems

These few poems are from the original 1,673 page manuscript *The Dark Bark* found buried in "The Yard" (as the poor animals who are to be euthanized call it) at the pound in Brighton Beach. They are the work of Rin Tin Tin. I write elsewhere of the strange and tragic events that led me to this manuscript—my depression, initial contacts with the spirit world, inadvertent destruction of the complete posthumous poems of Shakespeare as communicated to me by the spirit Elizabeth Barrett Browning, the establishment of communication with the dead animal world (Thank you, Ted Hughes) and, finally communication with Rinty's spirit with the assistance of the KA of W.H Auden. Here I can only give the briefest sketch of Rinty's life.

We know about Rinty and the movies. I'll skip that. What is not so well known is that he was an excellent jazz guitarist. He met Billie Holiday in the Fifties. They fell in love. No one knew.

Intellectual love, of course. He goes mad with grief after her death and—because all dogs know the essential existentialist insight—decides to create himself anew by joining the Cuban revolution.

It doesn't work—he tries to establish serious theatre in Cuba and overcome the typecasting he has suffered from all of his life.

Oh, during the first flush of revolutionary joy audiences accept him (he thinks) as Puck in his Marxist version of *A Midsummer Night's Dream*, but soon he is reduced to playing bit parts in proletarian dramas and then it's not long before there is no place for him in the State Theatre.

He works as a street performer for a bit—usually as Lenin—for the Soviet visitors Castro welcomes to the island. But then is arrested for anti-revolutionary activity when he tires of doing Lenin and tries a stint as Trotsky. After his release he makes his living—such as it is—teaching the mambo to canine candidates for the

Cuban National Circus and peddling marijuana to vacationers from Bulgaria.

In '66 he makes his move and escapes to NYC disguised as Chiquita Banana (he never says what happened to the young girl on the cruise ship who had been playing the part) and almost at once falls in with a crowd of drunken stand-up-comic wannabes and, while stoned and driving a dune buggy along the beach, runs down and kills poet Frank O'Hara.

(O'Hara died of injuries he received when he was hit by a vehicle on the beach at Fire Island, on Long Island, New York).

He flees to Cuba.

He is caught and sentenced to prison again where he is released by Castro—one of the hardened criminals Castro sends to the US—where, after many adventures, he attains his dream and is acclaimed as the "Hamlet of his Generation" by NY theatre critics. He gives it all up again and travels in Texas and Mexico playing country guitar and getting in fights arguing over whether Fredric Remington or De Kooning is the best artist. Gives that up and moves back to NYC. His poetry begins to be known.

The reader will note that in one sequence of poems Rinty claims to have assassinated JFK. True, he did testify before the Warren Commission but I believe we can dismiss these claims as sheer fantasy caused by Rinty's failure to get Leslie Howard's role in *The Manchurian Candidate*. I believe we should choose to remember the famous *Life* cover of Rinty saluting the eternal flame at JFK's tomb rather than those photos taken later that night on the Mall—drunken, under arrest and wearing only a significant leer and a leopard-skin pillbox hat.

Rinty spent his last years in New York City.

And then, of course, destroyed by his own loathing of his being in time as a dog all he has left—loveless and writing this memoir in the pound in Brighton Beach where he will be euthanized—are memories of his betrayals and regrets that overwhelm everything else.

Joe Green

The first poem "Late for a Poetry Reading" starts somewhat toward the end.

LATE FOR A POETRY READING

Late for a poetry reading
and trusting the Sufi
livery cab driver
because he pretended
he knew me
("How old are you
anyway? What is that
in dog years?")
and half drunk
in any case
having known
intellectual love
with Billie
She dead these
thirty years
and fame and
an excess of revolutionary
ardor those years
in Cuba
and don't even
ask me about the Sixties
having ridden the
Union Pacific
to the Cheyenne cutoff
loveless
in America
in winter

dreaming a
heavenly chasm
but no and
then hating
death and all
those who love it
returning through
West Texas from
Pancake to
Goodnight
in the railroad yard
there I heard
the OJays and
so returning to New York
and ending that night
somewhere in
I think
Long Island
poetry reading
in the Bronx
and at dusk
trying to find
my way back
seeing at the
window of
a perfectly bourgeois
house her a
young German Shepherd
the cream gold
glittering of her
eyes she looking
at this old dog

Joe Green

in perfect indifference
and knowing never
again I turn
the corner
always forever
going no-where
at the end of this
life

and bark
at the difficult dark.

This second poem is a beginning and an ending of sorts (a typical denouement) after Rinty returns to the USA after exile in Cuba.

Los Marielitos

You know Elmore Leonard
got a lot of his Florida schtick from me
when I was sobering up down in Miami.

I guess it was inevitable that I would
get involved with the mob after I fled Cuba
but it didn't start out that way.

May, 1980. They called us *Los Marielitos*.

I was one of 123,000 new Cuban refugees
that came to the USA in a short five months,
including about 5,000 of us who
were said to be hard-core criminals.

They crossed the ocean on a prayer.

On crowded, unsafe fishing boats.

On rafts held together by tires.

In search of a myth. Carrying only the
clothes on their backs, a passport, and a
crumpled piece of paper with a relative's phone number in the US.

I knew better.
The myth was over for me long ago.

Joe Green

I had Lassie's phone number but of course I would never call it.
She was probably dead and it was a whole new generation and
here I was, the icon of a previous generation, puking half-
    digested red beans over the side of a raft.

Back in the USA. Back in the USA
done in by the hype back then and by,
yes, my own yen to do serious theatre.

THE DEFIANT ONES

The studio really wasn't happy with Tony Curtis
His real name?
Bernie Schwartz.

They came to me. As always.

But I didn't really think it would be a good move
to play a role in which I would have
to be manacled to another actor for the whole movie.

I didn't tell this to Billie.
But she would have understood.
We had that kind of relationship.

"Don't threaten me with love, baby.
Let's just go walking in the rain."

I was already leery of typecasting
and ready to break out.

This was in '58, of course.
Billie died next year.
I remember what she told me:

"You can be up to your boobies in white satin,
with gardenias in your hair and no sugar cane
for miles, but you can still be working on a plantation."

Yeah, so my TV show was a hit.
So what?

Joe Green

West Side Story had been a possibility
It's based on *Romeo and Juliet*
but I turned that down too.

They didn't know about me and Billie.
Lady Day.

No one did.

If they only knew.

Sidney Poitier was a gentleman to me when
I met him but I felt that … well …
that he simply wasn't up to the role

and I was tired of having to carry my part
and everyone else's.

I suggested Richard Burton—a little makeup
… but they wouldn't go for it.

Sir Lawrence Olivier would have been good
But tell you the truth I didn't want to be chained to a lisping
    Limey for hours on end.

And I'll tell you what.

It was Shakespeare or nothing.
That's the way I felt.
I told Billie I loved her.
She said:

"Don't threaten me with love, baby.
Let's just go walking in the rain."

Joe Green

No, I Am Not Prince Hamlet Nor Was Meant To Be

You humans are so predictable.
In fact for years most dogs
were convinced that you were utterly
without self-consciousness—without Mind.

After all, we present a stimulus to you
and we ALWAYS get a predictable response.

The fact is we have such a horror
of the fact
that we can NOT be sincere
that we do whatever we can
to make it stop.

Yeah, a dog will pant
and bark and bring the
damn ball back again and again and again

—we do it to keep from going mad,
to hope to experience
just for an instant unmediated
unironic consciousness, to—for just one instant
—be THERE, be in the moment.

It never works.

Never.

That's why we die so young
and it is also why I was,
on a foggy evening OFF OFF Broadway
in a little theatre in the year 1959,

I was, simply put,

the best Hamlet of my generation.

Joe Green

New York City—Toward Night

When I reflect how that
My little light went out
Then I find my mind returning ever
To the Golden Retrievers
Of Manhattan
Forced into the indignity
Of limping beside
The jogging wife
Of the Day Trader
With her highlighted tresses
And DKNY shirt
And her pierced low-carb belly
Exposed and that bitter breed
Chained next to her
Desiring only, perhaps,
To die
Then only then
Am I at peace with Death.

In Loneliest Country

In Loneliest Country
I remember that
The philosopher Berdyaev wrote
About how when he
Was little and it was night
And he was with his mother
Wanting to get to Moscow
In a bolshoy hurry whizzing under
The stars in a sleigh the kind
Dear to the memory of Nabokov
That is a sort of unreal sleigh
As he was whizzing past all
Those wretched villages maybe
Seeing only a dog shivering
Before some wretched hut that
He thought "All over.
All over. No More. All lost."
He would never see that dog again.

But I was worried there
In Loneliest Country
Coatesville, PA turning
The corner of Second Avenue
Noticing a three-legged dog
Following me and seeing it all
Someone's dead grandmother
Passed me and I was looking
For the Loneliest Ranger wondering who is
That lonely and restless man
Behind that swinging façade?

The dog following me the American Icon
And no Mister though
You never asked you smoking
A Pall Mall in front of the
Furniture store across from
Lipkins I don't need a 21-Inch
Magnavox Color TV or a bedroom soot.
And where was Loneliest I'll bet
In Cuernavaca or Taxco
Up the street I am wearing my
Sheep shirt the one with all
The sheep on it. Damn dog.
Turning up the "Knowledge of Death
Is the Source of our Praise Avenue."
Unreal city and there he is
But I don't even have to ask
He says "Behind that swinging façade
Is another swinging façade." And then
"Do you remember the little cake shop
On the Neva the one Pound mentions
Where he never was where I never was
Where you never was" and I say
"Damn right I do."
And he is gone and I turn to
The little three-legged dog
Running TOWARD me and
I am happy and call
"Here, Hoppy! Come here, boy!"

1953

1953 was a hard year for me.
Sad. I don't know why.
I had work. Me and Bob Mitchum
Were friends at last. After all
Those misunderstandings. "You want to
Break out?" I asked him. "Then forget
All this crap about being a natural actor."
I took his drink away. Got his attention.
"Acting is a craft. Don't scowl at me.
You know I'm right. You'll never
Do Shakespeare unless ..." He eyed me warily.
"Yo, Rinty," he said. "You have Billie"
(I had told him) "What do I have?"
He fired up another Chesterfield.
Squinted through the smoke.
"Nothing happens anyway."

Nothing happens?
I knew what he meant.
I was getting there.

He grinned. "How the Hell did you
Do that to McCarthy?"
I gave him back his drink.
"Told him I was a commie, that's how.
"I'm an American Icon, Bob. It was too much for him.
Goodbye Tailgunner Joe."

Bob laughed but he didn't believe me.
He was really quite a charming man

Guys who don't believe in anything often are.
So he could be a gentleman to Rita Hayworth
Down in Mexico, her mind gone. But …
A bastard to everyone else.
Nothing in his eyes.

And I was sad there.
It was New York. September 13, 1953.
Another dive, another gig.
Bob left with a blonde before I began to play.
I started to play but just walked out.
It was the night Jimmy and Tommy Dorsey had
Finally gotten together again.
They kept playing while I put down my guitar.

They never forgave me.

"A" train to Harlem.
Got in Billie's DeSoto and drove.

In a few hours
Lost in Pennsylvania.
Stopped. Don't know why.
Got out. Looked up. Falling star.
Not me. Something from forever.

Finally found a town.
Asked a little guy outside a hospital for directions.
"We just had a baby girl," he said.

I drove back to my life.

L.A. Song

It's all pre-need as they say.
I knew it when I went to L.A.
To lend my peculiar grace
To that particular place.
I'm sorry that I had to stay.

It's the wanting it all that kills.
Still, I wish I had one of them stills
Of me "In the Yukon"
With that little toucan.
I'll never see it and no one else will.

I had a few drinks with my pals.
We wished we knew more of those gals.
Those gals who are sad
And wasted and bad.
The gals who were just like my pals.

So I stay in the Hollywood Hills.
And dream of the ghosts of those pills.
The kind you would take
At the Sir Francis Drake
And wait while the emptiness fills.

Joe Green

Breakfast at Tiffany's

And Capote there. Drunk in the morning.
That light is really what I remember
Through the window the jewels there.
Who was he anyway? Killings in Kansas.
"This is big, Rinty. I'm going to write about it.
Something new. Show them all."
Looking around tee he
To see who else was there.
Me looking at that light
"Look. Are you going to interview me or not?"
"A whole family. They killed them all.
Look I have a picture."
"I'm not looking at that," I said
And I was gone.

* * * * * * * * * * * * *

We were talking about Indians.
At the highway rest stop
You saw a stellar jay
Flying into the dark.

All these towns built on the bones
Of sleepy children!
Families hauling European clocks
Over the hourless prairie.

Into the dark again and the moon.
We stop even though it is below zero.
Something blows through our bodies.
Ghosts fleeing us. They can do this easily.

Tonight we finally see our bodies.
The moon's moon floats in the sky.
All night this happens!

* * * * * * * * * * * *

What do you hear on the radio radio?
What do you hear on the radio, dear?

* * * * * * * * * * * *

It was Christmas on Fifth Avenue
Ghost dog. Ghost dog.
I do this a lot.
I would save them all if I could.

Then I remember I left Capote with the check.
And I am happy again!

The green so green tree at Rockefeller Center.
Some guy telling a joke.
And I'm still hungry.
A Reuben and an egg cream.
The little waiter looking like God
His wife dead
Everyone a stranger forever.

Joe Green

What a Little Moonlight Can Do

Three days after Bastille day
Behind the shut-up café
In a broke-down car
(Hard to gas yourself
If the car won't start)
In Cross Plains, Texas
Thinking I saw nothing
More than myself
Reflected in my Les Paul
Black Beauty that night
I step out of my 1971
Ford Maverick the
Door operated courtesy
Light snicking on and
Look up at the sky
At all the tired animals
Stars bluewhitelonely
Thinking of that night
At the Three Deuces so
Long Ago and playing at
The Famous Door
The night Billie died
Errol Garner, Me, Oscar
Pettiford, Errol saying
You better than Django
But nobody will ever say it.
Not knowing Billie was dead
I was happy. Looking up
I say at the skyey animals
The old dog in the moon

Ending like this
Saying to the drunks
In the cowboy bar
This riff is based on *Les Négres*
By Jean Genet laughing
At myself really and now
Wanting it to end but
The car won't start. Looking
Up I remember I told Billie
Radiance is the dealbreaker
And heard, radio definably off
Her singing "What a Little
Moonlight Can Do" and
That was the last time
I was truly happy and
I was there knowing
I would never try
To find the music again

Tired.

Pancake

Levelland

Mule Shoe

Sonora

Meadow

Joe Green

What vistas of hidden forgetfulness
Exhaustively at hand!

After the First Death, Well ...

The collies yapped outside the funeral home
The whole world it seemed was sinking, sinking
I illumed the lamp, read a curious tome
Minnie Cheevied it and kept on drinking.
Damned hard to do with the goblins chuckling.
Ah, yes they won't get no satisfaction.
No swoons, or faints, and no knees buckling:
I read, and drink and choose inaction.
"More Ovaltine?" Lassie draws near.
"And tell me, Rinty, what are you reading?"
"It's only *Captain Midnight*, dear
Poor guy, he's taking quite a beating."
I kissed her, then said, "I won't forget
Though really screwed, he's not dead yet."

Joe Green

ROAD KILL

I ignore them.
The possum squashed on the macadam.
The unprophetic groundhog, in Texas
A holocaust of armadillos, the skunk
"Skunk. God!" you say.
Driving on, a snake absolutely flat on the road.

There is no heaven of animals
A rabbit. A black and white cat.
A small dog stinking in the sun.

You see them and you make up a story.
The dog setting out to warn us all:
Fire, fire in the forest! The turtle there
100 years old! … what thoughts there, Rinty?
And what innocence for all of them.

I'm glad one of us knows the signs
To find our home.

The Thing

The Thing that
Is really
Quite unrepresentable
I represent anyway
It's really
Quite tenable
Just like a lawyer
Whose client
Unkennable
Testified awfully
Horribly unmendable
Admitting something
Really unpennable
An unkennable, unfencible
Horrible thing.
Really quite venerable
Completely unlexible
Sadly unhexible.
You say that I represent nothing at all?
Please, make yourself comfortable.
I'll go make a call.

Joe Green

Rin Tin Tology

I never met Django
Never really wanted too, I guess
We would have "eyed each other warily"
Like the time I met Senator Jack Kennedy
Was it '57?
In the Cozy Cole me playing there
Jack with Sammy
Sammy told me he was nervous.
Jack working on his charisma thing
And me … height of my fame
Billie there Jack wanting her to come to his table
Her not noticing and me looking at her
Playing "*Vous et Moi*"
Sammy said "Man, come on down see who's here."
So afterwards I sit down next to the Senator
He in black glasses smoking a Kool
Undercover or something
Billie came over. She said she liked the man
Afterwards, knew his daddy … called him
Mr. Death. "That boy has troubles."
She said. "He was just nervous meeting me."
I told her. She could see that.
Anybody could. "He eyed you warily
Behind those shades" We laughed.
Forgot about it. I had something he wanted.
And he had something … something …
Held back … connection to … as if he knew
About us, about me and Billie,
Something he said. Joking about Howard Hughes.
Sammy told me Jack laughed afterwards.

"Said he was nervous. Something strange. Didn't
Know why."

In '63 in August Castro "eyed me warily."
A little moonlight, bourbon on his breath,
Backstage, the little moon a paper one
For *A Midsummer Night's Dream*. A wood near
Athens and I had transformed it, a bit of Brecht,
All of Shakespeare, Theseus nervous knowing
That Quince knew, Flute knew, Bottom breaking
the frame, declaring the revolution and me as Puck
Leaping, flying off that stage, like Peter Pan
TO FIDEL he standing up, smiling,
Me kneeling with the flowers but he
Afterwards backstage distant and cold wondering I thought
If the applause was for him or me.
Che was very nice, however.
Speaking one word … one word.
And I was in Dallas next was in Dallas then.
If I could play great jazz guitar
No hand … only paws.
Why couldn't I
Slowly, hold breath, there he is
Pull the trigger
Of a Manlicher-Carcano 6.5mm rifle?

Joe Green

The Platinum Goddess

Stepping into
Her room
I see
What should
Not be seen.
Beauty is sleeping.
Beauty is sleeping.
Nice work, my friends.
In Texas
Driving through
West Texas there
Ahead a silver trailer.
"Good Sam Club."
A dolt with a halo.
Passing on
The shoulder going

Nowhere I look up.
American dolt behind
the wheel.
Going nowhere.
Like me.
I can do nothing for him.
Arlington
Me standing before
The eternal flame.
Photogs.
Speed graphic cameras.
One tear.
Saluting Jack.
"American Icon"
Cover of *Life*
Yes, one wants life.
Nou goeth sonne under wod.

Joe Green

Boulez, Bloch, Maurice Ravel

Boulez, Bloch, Maurice Ravel
Tell me. Are you doing well?
I seem to hear a faint demurral.
Is that you?
Or just this squirrel
Shivering in my winter garden
While I stand here like Sydney Carton?

Mercy for all in fall of sparrow?
Do I hear a faint *Boléro*?

Letter from a Dog Before Troy

Dear Penelope,
It's windy here. Nine years in a tent on the beach.
Ulysses says they know what they're doing.

Right.
Nine years and for what?
What's nine years to them?
Most of my life.
I'm tired. Don't even ask me about the gods.
There's a limit to loyalty.
But you already know that.
I know about the puppies.
You should have told me.
She told me, of course.
I don't care.
Just get them out of Ithaca.
By the time you read this
I'll be gone. I have … what … four more years?
Going to someplace where there are no men.
No gods.
Maybe a few rabbits.

Joe Green

All the Starry Animals

Looking up
I love them too—
All the starry animals.
Looking down
Or not.
Not saying anything.
Not saying nothing either.

Old Dog: A Villanelle

I am an old dog and am gently trying,
To meekly go to the difficult dark.
Alone, alone I am slowly dying.
The slow snow drifts down and no wind sighing.
Take out a Zippo and light up a Lark.
No regrets none. No who and no whying.
Sad ghosts outside I hear them all crying.
Mort Sahl's on TV. Makes a funny remark.
No, thanks Time/Life I guess I'm not buying.
Death's at the door. The bastard is lying.
"Hey, Rinty! It's Lassie!" One small sad bark.
Wilder wind now. The snowflakes are flying.
Good Night has come. There is no denying.
Unknown is that country. Stark is the bark.
I am an old dog and am dying, dying.
And you, who haunt me forever sighing,
Crying my name in the difficult dark.
I am an old dog and am dying, dying.
I am alone and am dying, dying.
I am an old dog and am dying, dying.
I am an old dog and am dying, dying
Alone, alone I am slowly dying
I am alone and am dying, dying.

Joe Green

I Died In New York

I died in New York
At the shelter in Brighton beach.
My last silence.
I thought of Pound at Rapallo in the last years.
Silence. He didn't speak to anyone.
He too had been in a cage.
Like him I wrote and wrote
It was all I had left.
1,673 pages of my life.
And this is how it ends.
The guy gave me part of his pastrami sandwich.
I had Lou Reed's number.
I had Woody's.
But I didn't ask the guy to call.

"Come, kindly death," I wrote.
Not without irony. it's a line I never got to say.
The kind of line that went to others.

I acted with my body one arf one twitch of the tail
and you knew what it meant to be with the 7th at Little Big
      Horn your little boy dead beside you with a hole in his
      neck and the bright blood and the blue sky above and

the

red

Indian

yowling and you running to tell someone, tell Custer
tear his throat out for he brought you to this
and then they'd say "CUT" and I would have a smoke and mess
    around with my stand-in and tell Jew jokes and then

I

WAS

ON

but I never even began to be what I was

Never

Never

Never

and yes I could have been Lear.

Oh you are men of stone!

But I said not a word.

It's cold with the breeze from the beach.
I was in Brighton Beach
I was dying.

At Sardi's in '57 I think with Capote I told him
everything Hollygolightly and he took it and

changed the name to Tiffanys just because no one would believe a dog could be so tender and gay....

But I loved the movie.

It was cold in Brighton Beach
The guy also gave me some knishes.
All of it lost. I should have been kinder.

At night I howled.

My Epitaph

How oft has the Banshee cried
O'er a poor dead dog's grave?
Snow. Silence. Don't ask why.
Nothing to save.
Yet, I loved you sweet passers-by.
Dear Catchers in the Rye.
As you are so once was I.

Joe Green

Jazz Life/Afterlife

I went to Hell.
Never looked back.
Already been to Texas.

Talk about "Le Jazz Hot."
They were all there.
Of course.
The Hot Club.

Like before … they were ghosts.

I remember that time in the Four Aces
Errol saying. "You on tonight, my man"
Without irony.
I knew what he meant.
Laying down a line like Judassilver.
Wanting it all never getting it.
Missing that one chord.

He meant I wasn't perfect.
So perfect. So trying … like we all did.
Him what … in a few years?
Dead.
Love in vain.
All in vain.
And not

There … not getting it all
Just missing.

Notes dying.
Only rain outside.

Talk about "Le Jazz Hot."
They were all there.
Of course.
The Hot Club.

Joe Green

Before Another Poetry Reading

1.

Just like Robert Lowell
Before he went definably mad
My "author" (let's call him Joe) steps off the plane
Where he is met
With greasy servility
By a nervous graduate student
Who notes
Shaky hands
Red eyes
Too many whiskeys.
Into the car
"Reception at five, sir!"
"Five o'clock in the afternoon?"
Where are the great finned cars of yore?
Passels of Passats … only …
Joe eyes him warily.
"Take me to the Old Aquarium!"
"But … where?"
"I need to see the Colonel."
Vonnegut on the car radio. Still alive then?
"South Boston. I wait
For the blessèd break."
"Where…?"
"Drive," he says and somehow
There.

2.

"I have been living at the Garden of Allah.
Yours, Scott Fitzgerald"

Then
in the Wordsworth Room
Of the Pierce Brothers mortuary
1941 720 West Washington Boulevard
Ghost Dog
Returning to where I never was
Where was I?
Scott there. No.
"His hands were horribly wrinkled and thin."
At 44: "He actually had suffered and died an old man."
Returning then. Dorothy Parker remembers Gatsby.
Says "Poor son of a bitch." to Scott Not Scott.
No there there as they say.
Seeing what? Mystery. Seeing what she wanted.
Ghost Dog.
"Scott, I will always remember looking in on
whatever it is that is to me, you.
Yours, Rin Tin Tin."

3.
At the monument.
Remembering that line about Shaw's father.
Looking for Loneliest there, perhaps.
Joe then back in the car.
"I'm ready," he says.
Shaky hands, red eyes..
"It's almost five. I don't know if we'll make it."
"Skunk hour," Joe thinks.
"Drive like the wind," he says.
Relinquunt Omnia Servare Rem Publicam.

Joe Green

Epigraph

I bark at the dark until the darkness yields.
As you go stark. Babbling of green fields.
Yours,
Rinty

From the Limerick Odyssey

Book Twelve

The Sirens, Scylla and Charybdis, the Cattle of the Sun

[The Crystal fretting of the Multiverse Impends, The Thunderwords, Ahab keeps on keeping on, The Gong-Tormented Sea]

If you're like me, you've been wondering
What's up with this incessant thundering.
Like Alice said:
Go feed your head.

You know there must have been a hundred
Cracks in the crystal fretting.
You won't lose if you're betting.
And if you're in the habit
Of following the white rabbit
You know there is no forgetting

Not really of the warp and the woof.
There's no holding yourself aloof:
You open the latch
And there's a bandersnatch
And things as they are go poof.

Datta. Dayadhvam. Damyata.

Joe Green

Or just in case you kinda forgot a
contransmagnificandjewbangtantiality
Of an alternate reality
A kind of extended fermata.

They all felt the lonely absurds
As they heard these thunderwords
Ahab looked out
Then shouted out
"Words! Words! Words!"

bababadalgharaghtakamminarronnkonnbronntonnerronntuonn
thunntrovarrhounawnskawntoohoohoordenenthurnuk

Perkodhuskurunbarggruauyagokgorlayorgromgremmitghundhu
rthrumathunaradidillifaititillibumullunukkunun

klikkaklakkaklaskaklopatzklatschabattacreppycrottygraddaghse
mmihsammihnouithappluddyappladdypkonpkot

And I thought I saw Leopold Bloom
There in an upper room
Of the Spouter Inn
With Finnegan.
Or how can I presume?

And Ahab leads each man-o
To Rick's Café Américain-o
Always seafaring
The awful daring
And besides he really liked Sam-o.

Ahab said, "Ok, play it again."
Odysseus said, I remember when
I was in a poem
And couldn't get home
We sailed back to Circe and then

She gave us some sort of advice.
"Don't look back. Don't think twice.
And remember what Byron
Said about the Sirens
Nothing else will ever suffice

But to put wax in your sailor's ears
As near the sirens they steer.
But if you want to hear them,
As you draw near them
Take all that nautical gear

The ropes and the chains and the padlocks
And fasten them to the oarlocks
And before the mast
Make yourself fast
You got all of that, Sherlock?

And then, perhaps, you can listen
As they sing of that one and this one
In immortal love
Sent from above
And how their dear bones glisten

In a cave beneath the sea
They are calling, they are calling to thee

And your sweet wife is drowned
And all around
Is strange beauty of the highest degree.

It will be the Deep Blue Goodbye
You'll want to live there and so you will die
Any pleasure you took …
The Long Lavender Look …"
She looked sweetly at me. Did sigh.

So ho! for the Empty Copper Sea.
My stout crewmen and me.
A Tan and Sandy Silence
Without ideals, without violence
And, oh! The difference to me.

We sailed through The Lonely Silver Rain.
Rain then sun again:
One Fearful Yellow Eye
In the Dreadful Lemon Sky
Then again The Lonely Silver Rain.

The wind was a Turquoise Lament
Darker Than Amber the evenings that sent
The meteor's Free Fall in Crimson
And the inexpressible frisson
Of leaning against the mast and smoking a Kent.

We sailed into the Horse Latitudes
As I strove to correct their attitudes
A knowing ennui
Is just the thing for the sea

And a knowledge of the sailor's beatitudes.

But my men lacked the bel esprit
For which I had the master's degree
They brought out the rope
But I had little hope
"I do not think they will sing to me."

But they sang to me like no other
And they sang to me of my dear brother
Travis McGee
On the wine-dark sea
But I'm Odysseus, so why did they bother?

"Come," they sang, "It's not far
To slip F-18 at Bahia Del Mar
And that's not all
Chookie McCall
Waits for thee at the built-in bar.
And Meyer is on the John Maynard Keynes
See how sweetly he leans
With the lovelychildren
And Puss Gillian
Nobody knows what it means.
Hear the seas sounds, the rush
Of the waters past the Busted Flush
In Time and In Space
A new and wonderful case
And the melancholy, expected hush
Of all beauty when you then arise!
What strange stars and strange skies
As the plot begins

Joe Green

With Boodles gin
And a solo by Sonny Rollins dies!"

I cried out. But I was ignored
They had wax in their ears heretofore.
I wanted to be
Travis McGee
And Odyssey here no more no more!

But we rowed past—all the lovely songs
As the Sirens shimmied in sexy sarongs
I was released
Then it was on to the beast.
The sea was tormented by gongs.

Oh, the gong-tormented sea-o
Dolphin torn like it's supposed to be-o
Whatever that means
It made for wonderful scenes
And damn fine poetry-o.

I had forgotten to tell my men
That it looked like six of them
We're gonna be dead
That's what Circe said
But I was only looking out for them:

For Charybdis it seemed quite certain
Would mean, for all of us, curtains
If we chose Scylla
That beastly Godzilla
Only six would be hurtin'.

She had six hungry heads-o
And never ever took her meds-o
And 18 sets of teeth
And breath that did seethe
With the mangled corpses of the dead-o.

So we went and rowed on past her
"Boys," I said, "You better row faster."
But it was no use
She sank each ugly tooth
Into the hides of six poor sad bastards.

When she took them they cried out to me!
But that's death on the dark copper sea.
And we wept
Drank and then slept
And came to Thrinacia by 3.

Of, course, Odysseus continued his story
But Homer got it all down before he
Got to this part.
The fellow lacked art.
So we won't get into it anymore he

Had as early as the first damn book
Told how the poor sailors cooked
The Oxen of the Sun
And when they were done
Were wriggling on Poseidon's hook.

And all about Odysseus and Calypso.
He did it facto ipso.

Joe Green

So we will conclude
This strange interlude
And take a few lingering sips-o

Of Boodles the Gin that's preferred
By Travis McGee. Have you heard?
John MacDonald is dead
That's what they said.
And I find it all very absurd.

Books Thirteen through Twenty-Four

[Hark! 'tis an elfin-storm from faery land,
Of haggard seeming, but a boon indeed:
Arise—arise! the morning is at hand;—]

Odysseus looked up. It was day.
The free French were singing "*La Marseillaise*"
Sam was asleep
And dark dreams did keep
Rick awake in the American café.

Outside the warp and woof trembled.
Overall you might say it resembled
What's going on
In the Gospel of John
And beings sentient and nonsentient assembled

In the sky above the Time and Space Port
Where possibilities of every sort
Reclaim transcendence
In a way that's quite splendid
Revoking the claims of *La Morte*.

"Away!" Ahab cried "The *Pequod*
Waits for us—nor other men nor gods
I'll continue my quest
But I think it is best
For you to go home. Damn it's odd.

And I think it's worth asking just why
You will live and I'll have to die
Because I rage against IS
The Nothingness Biz
While you long for your dear wife and sigh

And you are considered the wanderer
Though exposed as a poor blunderer
While my mission
Ends in Nuclear fission
Thundered Ahab the Asunderer.

And the Band played "The Leaving of Liverpool"
And Odysseus played "The Flop-Eared Mule"
And there was Grace
All over the place
Which is something you never learn in school.

Odysseus went aboard, fell asleep
And the *Pequod* made it over the deep,
And he still was snoozing
As they went cruising
Ahab said, "I have promises to keep."

Odysseus snoozed. They made land!
Ahab left him there on the strand
Beneath the Steel Pier
And he thought it quite queer
To awake to the strains of a Dixieland band.

And there in the air—A Flying Horse!
It wasn't Pegasus, of course
But a horse named José
Owned by Dennis O'Day
Who jumped with negligent force

From a Diving Platform right there
Then plunging through the salt air
Into a pool.
Nothing so cool
Had been in Ithaca *avant La Guerre.*

Now the plot is beginning to thicken:
On the boardwalk there is a chicken
That, well, you know,
Can play Tic Tac Toe.
On a bench Mr. Pickwick from Dickens

Looks out at the glowing salt sea-o
And who's passing by? Hey, it's me-o!
With my dear old dad
And I feel rather sad
There's something I want for me-o—

Another box of saltwater taffy
And a number of comics about Daffy
The Duck
But I'm having no luck.
For my father's had too much black cafee.

Joe Green

And it's father and son on a quest.
My father thinks it is best
At this late date
To micturate
At our hotel and then rest

In our rooms on Baltic Avenue
Yes, right there. What can you do
If you are the son
Of a son of a gun
Who's had too much caffe? You're through.

But you saw the old diving horse
And the Monster of the Sea, of course,
Will be on display
For just one more day
And your dad with irresistible force

Is dragging you through 1958-o
And, seeing that now I say Wait-o!
All that is gone
Keeps going on
The white rabbit tells you "You're late-o."

Ah, you still don't get the idea?
Well, Odysseus now begins his career.
But Vaudeville is dead
So George Burns said
"We better get outta here."

And Odysseus says "Where's my son?
And Telemachus came on the run
And then who did they see
But Penelope
Singing "Ain't We Got Fun."

They glide, they glide like ghosts
Past all readers with their broken remotes
Yes, they fled away
Just on that day.
They're gone. Didn't leave any notes.

Joe Green

Orson Welles Interviews Joe Green

ANNOUNCER: Ladies and gentlemen, the director of the Mercury Theatre and star of these broadcasts, Orson Welles.

ORSON WELLES: Hello, the Jeunesse Dorée and all the ships at sea and in the maelstromed starry welkin!
   This is ORSON WELLES.

Our interview tonight is with Joe Green. On this particular evening the Crosley service estimates that thirty-seven billion creatures, mortal and immortal, are listening to us on their Zenith Trans-Cosmic radios. Ratings are up, I see. Tonight we have a show I think you will enjoy. Poet and great actor/artist sit before the fire in the reconstructed redwood cabin nestled deep in the Carmel Valley hills under the famous Owl Oak, orgiastic abode of the muse. Outside an ill wind is blowing nobody good, but herein, where warmth and camaraderie hold sway along with John Powers and Johnny Walker, we are blessed with anticipatory frissions and make no bones about it. So make yourself comfortable with your favorite psychic aid and be prepared to be ... well, I'm not sure.... Mr. Green, or should I refer to you by another of your many monikers? Joe?

JG: Joe. Just Joe.

ORSON: Kevin Killian wrote: "Joe Green's poetry has a savage wit and a plaintive, enchanting innocence, like some of Joe Brainerd's drawings." Who is Joe Brainard?

JG: Some guy with a savage wit and a plaintive, enchanting innocence.

ORSON: Hmmm. You've had an interesting life haven't you? I wonder if you could tell us a bit about those experiences that most shaped your *weltanschauung*. Who were your formative influences and why?

JG: I went to Catholic schools in the doomed mill town of Coatesville, Pennsylvania. The town was haunted but, at the same time, I had access through books and, heartbreakingly, mostly through insights arrived at too late to supernal beauty. At six, my first day at St. Cecilia's I asked "Who signed me up for this?" Back then we were mostly doomed and had no idea what to do about it but there were moments of grace and immortal spirits in the "wanting them to be immortal spirits" sense who now exist in my memory. I want them to be remembered in my poesy but mostly can't even get close to what I would like to do. Only a few somehow exist as more than markers for a certain sense of rage and bafflement that my poesy now and then is lucky enough to express. I got out of there—the U.S. Army took me away.

I was reading Spinoza at ten. Absolutely true. Of course, I didn't understand a damn thing but the point was something else. Somehow—please tell me if I am wrong here, Orson—I got the idea there was a class system here in the good old USA and that the place was run mostly by madmen who contrived to also be very boring. Also I got the idea that they owned me. But I had nary an inkling that I could in fact ever know just how they got me or what I could do about it. The bigotry of low expectations. I also somehow developed a complete indifference to and a lack of interest in getting along—although I got along in the sense that I am still here. Most anyone I knew from there who had anything like an inkling to escape were ruined in all the usual ways. Escaped to the Army and death, drugs ... blah blah.

I knew a man—a boy—for example, who was a good artist.

But—just incidentally believed he just might be John Lennon. He went to NYC to become a junkie and then, while finding refuge on various street corners, stayed awake nights as much as he could drawing miniature street scenes on cardboard (scenes you have never seen) and somehow recovered enough to bring it all back home where, arrested and taken to the local prison, promised he would escape—beaten again—still made that promise, beaten more (and I have this account from others there—others whom I met years ago and almost passed in the street since who knew that the bums with no teeth were my old friends) just laughed. "You assholes," he said. "Can't you tell I'm kidding?"

That's poetry, by the way.

The old friends I met retold this to me and all laughed about it and then went into a long riff about how there aren't any cops around like the old cops and how much they missed them. So, Kevin got out and somehow stopped shooting heroin (is that phrase antiquated?) and kept drawing and who knows if he finally stopped but he died. Another friend (the great John Rollins) called me up and told me "We lost Kevin" and this struck me as such an odd want to be genteel and lost way to put it and this phrase came back to me as I in a half hour wrote a poem on my father's dying. That poem is "Last Night." "Absolute lucidity and purest, most marvelous bullshit" as a great poet said.

So where was I? Ah, in Coatesville. Sometimes I call it "Warrensville" in my poems. My way out (although I never got out) was books. Contrast me, Orson, with my friend Tim Smith who, at the age of 17, heard a neighbor playing a flamenco record, said yes and was on his way to Spain in an instant to learn to do just that. What a moron I was. I remember riding on a train to Philly seeing some cadets from Valley Forge Military Academy (exactly where Holden Caulfield escaped from) and longing to, at least, even be there. But I stayed.

But—books and so years of bellycrawling through stacks in libraries and somehow still back in Coatesville was enough since I was cursed with an imagination that monstered everything there with significance and a sense of the transcendent.

In other words, early on I stopped looking at the usual reality and made up my own movie. Is this a bad thing? You would know.

But I had all those books and ... let's be honest here. By the time I was 17 I had read—with a bit of the right sort of attention—most of the deathless poesy in English and there was bliss and I always had that and withal always had an unfortunate but needed distance from this our vale of tears. And then—being asked to leave a certain Jesuit university....

ORSON: Wait. The Jesuits expelled you?

JG: Yes, it was 1967. My roommate turned me in for smoking marijuana! He saved me from a life of addiction. I was summoned before the Dean and a panel of Jesuits. They told me they knew what I was doing. I never imagined they knew I was a marijuana addict, so I confessed to other heinous acts including building a snowman in the Joan of Arc chapel and stealing the scarf of a prominent poet invited to speak there. They concluded the inquisition. I was gone, baby, gone. Sent home. But then—I was lucky enough enroll in Lincoln University on a minority student scholarship where I was taught English Lit the good old way and loved it. All professors there were odd fellows and exiles. And then—let's pass years and years—I was damn lucky to do a doctoral program at the place where Berryman jumped—the professors there my friends equally in love with all that is there. The tales I could tell. And in any case there was a sense of the sacredness and absolute importance of scholarship (as in getting off your lazy ass and discovering something other than yourself and wanting truth) that was deepened which, along with a contempt for the pretense that kills that I got from growing up peculiar in a doomed mill town and a healthy hatred of systems of oppression embodied by the trivial and designed to protect them has brought me to your attention—perhaps the greatest artistic failure of the 20th century though you be imaginary and tra la la to that. As you understand.

ORSON: Of course. We'll skip over the rest I guess. The railroads, the Asian nights, the semi-furnished rooms, the carnival. What would you say your primary motivators are now?

JG: I don't know. I have always been desperate and confused and expect to continue being desperate and confused. No doubt and if I am lucky all will be revealed a moment or two before death. I am not a knower of myself or, perhaps, don't want to know. Of course I am desperate to stop time or, if that concession can't be made, to have enough time. Really, it's all in *The Tempest*, although I would like my wife along with my daughters on that island along with a few boon companions. My wife and daughters would have no problems with Caliban—they know much more than I ever will. So, no problem there … and I could fiddle about as I do and everyone would be safe.
But that won't happen.
I'll probably muddle along pretending it has. Anent poetry—it would be nice to have it occur as it once occurred.
And I would like a cabin in a bee loud glade—a great advantage there in Innisfree is that one can at times escape from the constant knowledge that one has to go through all these things twice.
No place for bad art in any case.

ORSON: You left Coatesville for the Army. After graduating from Lincoln?

JG: Yeah, got drafted. This was back when wars were really fucked up. But I managed to avoid Vietnam. I signed up for a third year in the Army and got sent to the Defense Language Institute in Monterey, California where I learned 19th-century Russian. The Army! Read my poems ... Jim Moore ... and the rest. Those were strange times. I refused to sign up for another year so I got sent to Fort Huachuca for the nine week course to be a POW Interrogator. Then they discovered we were not at war with Russia but we might be so I spent some time playing a Russian POW. The Green Berets would capture and interrogate me. My name was Lieutenant Jakov.

ORSON: C'mon.

JG: Absolutely true. We forget the good parts. After that I was set to Fort Hood where I was assigned to the Language Training Facility to teach English to the Korean, and Vietnamese and Japanese and German brides soldiers returned with from over there ... then I got out. For three months. Bad times. Was selling Kirby vacuum cleaners in Hollywood and so reenlisted and was sent to Fort Huachuca, met Charlie Solomon (see the poem about him) and landed a job writing Army manuals. The manuals "Combat in Built-Up Areas" and "Nuclear, Biological and Chemical Warfare?" They're mine.

Got out and went to Waco, Texas. I was determined to get a job so signed up to learn bricklaying at Texas State Technical Institute. But I am (as I was told by an instructor) a "spatial idiot" so I took electronics instead and then got a job as a technical writer in Dallas writing manuals for the Army. Yep! And I mean writing. I shared a desk with a guy who lived in a trailer with six miniature Dobermans and drank at least a fifth of vodka a day and we wrote everything in longhand to be typed by the poor women downstairs....

ORSON: And were you writing poetry?

JG: A bit. I always had. But then came Control Data.

ORSON: What?

JG: Yes, got a job there in Dallas writing the first "online" learning for the PLATO system. That system ... mainframes linked each to each ... was a sort of pre-Internet. We created the first online Forums. I created one called "Poetry." Tim Smith was working at Fort Ord in a "learning lab" and had access to the system. We both began posting poems. Some of the poems were written by Samson Shillitoe who was posting from an insane asylum in Mexico. We were believed! My wife-to-be, Connie, was living in Minnesota and had access to the system. She saw through me. I fell in love. I flew out to Carmel, California and met Tim. We made the Parapark Tapes and began the collaboration and fun that is still going on. Pretty soon I wangled a transfer to Minnesota. Connie and I were married. Once there I gained access to the USENET as I was working for CRAY Computer. I began posting in newsgroups there and "met" great ones. Those were the days, my friend. Through those connections my poetry began to be known. Kinda ...

ORSON: Now I know you've been translated into Russian and that the prestigious if impecunious poets at Fulcrum magazine admire your work. But let's begin with something from your past, "The Insect Clerks of Neiman Marcus." I invited C.G. Jung to join us to discuss this seminal work, but he was unable, being called away to answer Freud's claim that he was a mere occultist. Please sir, what is this "'new mythology" of which you speak and how does the poem embody it?

JG: I have no idea, Orson. A vile paraphrase (and there's no avoiding that) would say this and that but really what happens is that everything happens at once and that phrase allows or creates or whatever the "small, blue clouds" weeping or the "indifferent mandibles" and the rest and there is nothing like it.

I noticed that when I said "nothing like it" there was flash of merriment on your own immortal features. I suppose this is one of my many irritating qualities. That is, I know what a good poem is. It doesn't matter at all to me whether I wrote it or someone else just because it seems very odd in the most important way to even talk about an "I." Anyone who has ever written a good poem is completely unable to tell you how the poem was made. How could they? They have no damn idea. Too bad. So, occasionally, damn you, someone comes along who gets lucky once in a while a writes a good poem (not a great one) and can tell when a poem works and when it doesn't and is, yes, right.

ORSON: Jung told me that this was one of his favorite poems that it accomplished what he was attempting to do with his ideas of "active imagination," that is, the manifesting of archetypal images and their energies by allowing one's psyche to emerge from behind the super-ego's judgments. He was particularly fond of your choice of names for the psychopomps Buffy, Megan et. al. Can you say a bit about why those names were chosen and what you hoped to accomplish there? Is Jung right that this what you intended?

Joe Green

JG: I wrote this in the eighties but I continually renew my acquaintance with these psychpomps.

ORSON: Let's turn to a more recent work. Of "Bell, Book and Candle" one reviewer wrote: "He has one poem about Kim Novak and James Stewart in *Bell, Book and Candle* that perfectly expressed the Technicolor genius of Richard Quine, that films unsung genius director." Now, as a cinematic soul myself, I can see this. But, and of course you may disagree, what does this have to do with your particular way? How does the cinematic image affect what you do as an artist?

JG: It was Kevin Killian who said that. Wonderful fellow! Yes, there you are in the dark gazing at a flickering image and somehow your eye must go there and then there, pull back, close up, and so on and before it was done in the movies it was done in poetry but who gets this really? I know you did and—we can talk about this later—that you know that Shakespeare invented the movies (oh, along with Marlowe and Cyril Tourneur and the rest). It's all of a piece and I noticed this and wrote about it, half understanding, when I wrote about all those speeches in the Bard's plays that are little narratives within the larger narrative. And somehow this is something I can somehow sometimes do. One of the blisses of this poem about movies (and masques and revels—the knowing reader will find a way to see this—allusion again and used in a merry way) is that it works like a movie. Close up to Jimmy's silver cigarette lighter and his shaky hand, the witch hangs an ornament on the tree and she knows she knows what you are looking at, last shot—snow steepling the Chrysler building and that impossible movie moon all framed just so, music swells and then ... Ha!

And have you asked about my masterpiece? I have one even

as the most neglected poet as recognized by the great souls of the Russian steppes and wedding cake academies must have one. It's "The Diamond at the End of Time" in all its splendid not anything like it a hell of a lot of fun and worlds there yes glory and it is one hell of a movie. Cuts, fades, swirling images, sailing aways, Fairbanks and Flynn and a damned fine fight scene.

So, yes, it's all about the movies.

ORSON: Cats figure prominently in your work, Joe. From Pyewacket Tallpockets padding through halls, to the creations of Hitler's Cat, you've created your own feline fantasies. It's been said that cats are images of the unity of opposites: loyalty and independence, affection & aggression, playfulness & dignity, curiosity & indifference, earthy sensuality and an otherworldliness. Is this search for wholeness or reunification a theme in your life and work?

JG: Thanks, Orson. Glad you reminded me. I need to pick up some Friskies Hairball Control cat food tonight. Let me see if I can remember:
>
> Puddytat
> Joey
> Abe
> Mean Man
> Foo Foo
> Iggy
> Sarah
> Sparkle
> Spicoli

You're right about me and cats. As long as the cat come home. And cats have a sense of humor. I think there's a mannerism of solemnity that is pervasive in contemporary poetry that people mistake for gravitas. Somebody said that. Cats won't put up with that.

I mean, I have written poems as Hitler's Cat. Do you find Hitler's cat in a poetry workshop or lecturing at this and that conference by the sea? No—too much respect for himself and a sense of the absurd that prevents it. You know—there are a lot of questions contemporary poets should ask themselves and one is "What would Mehitabel do?"

Would Mehitabel reprehend a comic persona as the silly fellows so serious do? No.

And, Jesus, Orson you were a great actor. What do you make of legions of "creative" people who never assume a role, never act, don't know what to do with, for example, the gifts Rin Tin Tin offers just as an example? Or—this leads to bigger questions. What little joy and what can be done about it? The universe is bursting with giant forms and this is what we get? Or the absurd and unlikely and blissome ridiculous is everywhere offering an escape from the dwimmer of the dreary—and they can't find it?

A certain sort of "seriousness" is imitated everywhere. Sadly, when a comic poem is attempted the "poem" part is missed. That is, the comic poem lets slip the surly bounds of ordinary comedy also—there is a move to touch on a higher mirth, an uncommon wit, something free and of itself.

Hell, you know that. You understood Falstaff.

I sense some inkling of the comic and poetic in the lower realm of internet poetry. Some role playing—with, mostly, nothing of the divine and blushful Hippocrene. The higher one ascends though the spheres of contemporary poetry the less chance there is of any glimmer of comic stardust. A cat won't put up with that.

I think I already said this: a great poem eludes systems and ideologies. And, just because it does, it is continually placed within systems and ideologies by its cultured admirers and despisers alike. But certain admirers can read a great poem and see that their apprehension of it is incomplete and thrill to that just because it seems to point to an Outside. Of course, this is just how I feel and I am guy who misses reading essays such as "Milton and the Pendant World" or "The Two-Handed Engine: Sheep hooks, Blind Mouths and the Regii Sanguinis Clamor." And also I am a very sentimental fellow.

Of course we are not chatting about deconstruction in my post festum definition: "The *L'espacement* of the *Aufhebung* that ravishes—under a "false" appearance—absence that—*toujours déja perdu*—re-presents itself as the copula between Being and Becoming.

Or are we?

ORSON: We haven't spoken much of your Doctoral project. It's not often that an academician wanders the road less taken as you have. How would you characterize your love of The Bard and your academic interest in his works, and how does that square with your creative opus?

JG: Orson, you loved Shakespeare above all and above all characters loved Falstaff so you already know that there is more of beauty and terror and wonder and freedom in Shakespeare than anywhere else. Others abide the question etc. He's the most mortal of poets—simply because his immortal longings make the strongest claim ever but are forever denied. So, attention must be paid. Well of English must be kept undefiled and all that.

It's probably a secret that only a minority in most English departments actually give a rip about poetry. It's been that way since the beginning. There are so many other ways (all the loathsome schools of criticism) to make one's way. And only a remnant in any case anywhere have a feeling for poetry. So, for example Professor Donald Foster 12 or so years ago alleged that his computer study (word frequency etc.) revealed that Shakespeare was the author of a certain Funeral Ode.

It was impossible to believe this if you had a sense for poetry. The fact that under the hideous Stephen Greenblatt the ode was admitted to the Norton is a tragicomic tale. But there it is.

Now, of course, Wallace admits a hideous mistake. But back in the beginning I was there with others of the remnant bashing him on the head. We finally got through. Jesus H Christ. And Greenblatt is the author of a best selling "Life" of the Bard. The point is that if Shakespeare needs protection from the barbarians at the gate we are all in danger. And I've met the best guardians in academia—sneaking a smoke in their office, hiding from the department chairman, worrying if Milton really saw Shakespeare, spending their lives to establish a better text of "King Lear," dying in mysterious fires or—when the gods are with them—establishing their own departments in which they are the only member. Regents Professors at last!

More or less this. I've known people who have given their lives over to a real quest for truth and for some flash of real poetry transmitted through them so.... And the real mortal stakes are, sadly, elsewhere and lives are crushed every day by this sort of getting along. Poetry is whatever gets said in spite of systems of tyranny that seek to prevent the saying. Real academicians do what they can to speak through these systems and point to what is there.

Besides, they are my best audience for layers of wild and comic allusion. And somebody has to make them, for a second, kind of happy.

ORSON: When I was working on Citizen Kane, I often found myself staying up late and reading Yeats to settle me down. As a fellow Irishman, what do you and Yeats have in common?

JG: The colder eye. Just kidding. Ok, so let me be explicit. Here's what once happened.

I was in this multiverse, see? And I met this Chevalier named D'Arc and he lived in a sort of space ship. He used to collect universes.

"You collect … universes?" An interesting hobby I thought.

"Oh, not any more. We don't have the room. But look—isn't that an interesting one?"

I'd seen better. There was something strange about the universe in the snow globe. I sipped my Martini and tried to think of just what it was. It was much as you would expect. It seemed mostly empty but here and there one could detect tiny bits of phosphorescence which were of course unimaginably huge clusters of galaxies containing billions and billions (as poor Carl Sagan used to say) of intelligent entities. The glow is the thing I learned later. Red is bad. A brilliant blue is best. This universe overall gave the impression of a rather pale red. Ten being the highest—it was, perhaps, a three.

"That universe lacks … pep."

"Exactly," D'Arc cried. "And do you know what universe this is?"

I glanced around the room. I knew what was coming. I felt quite restless.

"It's yours!" he cried.

He seemed to be expecting something.

The Chevalier put a slim finger on the boring universe. And grinned.

"Of course it isn't."

All three of us grinned.

"For Poetry yet lives!" we cried in unison.

And then me and Tim and Philip and Ben and Katia and John and Mark and Tara and Michael and … and many immortal poets I have been lucky to meet descended into the snowy streets of Manhattan! Singing "We Be Soldiers Three."

The Manhattan of Dreams! Chatted with Gene Kelly. Went to the pre-Midnight Midnight mass at the Basilica of St. Gladys de la Croix on Washington Heights. And despite our audience's inevitable protestations, and equally inevitable disappointment, I cannot be expected to make any attempt to describe, in words, the sound of the Elhanan Q. Hackenback Memorial Grand Pipe Organ in the Basilica of St. Gladys de la Croix on Washington Heights. The task is beyond me.

Remember? You were there too, Orson! Remember? By 11:30 we were seated and somewhat drunk in the rather fabulous first-class lounge of the Fredonian-owned but German-flagged Zeppelin, the *Arthur Schopenhauer*. Both Will and Idea were expressed in the furnishings. A zinc bar, overhead various Teutonic maidens (carvings, of course) in various stages of undress. Nice idea. All in various states of yearning expressing the embodiment of the Will. It was cigars and schnapps then and a 22-piece orchestra playing selections from Mozart. We hardly noticed when we cast off. It was Christmas Day in 1927 in the Manhattan of Dreams in the 115th Weft of the Realm Agenath Hetaim—about 40 billion billion megaparsecs from Altair if you take a sharp left.

ORSON: Ah, yes … Hmmmm.… As we're nearly out of time here, I want to say how grateful I am to have had this opportunity to chat blithely with you, Joe. Ah, I hear the chimes at midnight! I hope we can speak together again. Anything you want to add

… or want to ask me before we indulge in these two bubbling glasses of Muscatel?

JG: I hope you seek out "The Limerick Homer." It's all of Homer translated into limericks by me and the immortal poet Tim Smith. You can find it by googling "The Limerick Iliad" and "The Limerick Odyssey." And …

ORSON: Thank you, Mr. Green; may your god go with you.

Acknowledgements

Fulcrum 2 (2003, Cambridge, MA) "What of it?" "Point Lobos 1944," "Just Spring with Chaucer and Some Shriners." "Old Father," "Dinosaur Love," "At the Hospital."

Fulcrum 3 (2004, Cambridge, MA) "Late for a Poetry Reading," "The Defiant Ones," "Francis of the City of St. Francis," 'The Diamond at the End of Time," "The Red Light Is The Blue Light Is."

Fulcrum 4 (2005, Cambridge, MA) "The Rain, "Ok, Then … So We Were in Fredonia," "Trio."

Fulcrum 5 (2006, Cambridge, MA) "The Ballad of Little Noddy," "Incident on 52nd Street," "Last Night," "I Think Continually of Those Who Are Truly Late," "Canarios—Or the Escape of D.B. Cooper," "Jim Moore," "My Demented Mother."

Fulcrum 6 (2007, Cambridge, MA) "Sonnet—The Sense of an Ending," "Dreamland," "The Iliad of Joe Green." "In 1953," "I Love Them Old Hippies," "Warrensville 2," "Warrensville 3," "In the Blue Note," "Negative Capability," "A Ballade," "In Loneliest Country."

Fulcrum 7 (2008, Cambridge, MA.) "I Look Out and I Hear the Knell," "The Ballad of Steve," "My Father in the Store Commanding 'Buy'," "Oh, Donna," "The Ballade of Susie Lamont," "The Ballad of Ernie White."

Rattapallax 12 (New York, NY) "A Lone Ranger Christmas," "Luftmensch."

Poems have also appeared in *The Diamond at the End of Time* (Owl Oak Press, 2006), *The Dark Bark: Poetry and Songs of Rin Tin Tin* (Owl Oak Press, 2006), *The Limerick Homer* (Owl Oak Press, 2008).

And eternal thanks to Marc Vincenz (who is NOT fictional but illumes Space and Time and anything else) for publishing these poems!

About the Author

Joe Green was born in Coatesville, Pennsylvania in 1948 and yet lives. As one can see from the picture of him as a young cowboy in this book he had big ears. He also attended St. Cecilia Catholic School back when attending Catholic schools was very very strange. His poem about Sister Eucharista dangling a kid out a second story window is true although the Blessed Virgin Mary did not visit his mother so they could drink and watch the Perry Como Christmas Special together.

Joe got his ears fixed in the sixth grade. Things did not improve. He went to Bishop Shanahan Catholic High School in West Chester where, among other accomplishments, he was caught reading Nietzsche during a prayer retreat. He had concealed *The Portable Nietzsche* in a *Lives of the Saints* cover. This was in 1963 during the Cuban Missile Crises. Father Schneider caught Joe reading Friederich while taking a break from looking out the window to see if the Soviet Union had yet sent missiles to obliterate the school.

Joe graduated in 1966 and went to Marquette University. He lasted there for one year and was then kicked out because of his marijuana addiction—which he somehow overcame. Disgraced and branded, he slunk back home where he was accepted into Lincoln University in spite of the fact that he had smoked something someone said was marijuana but he suspected was electrical bananas as in the Donovan song . Lincoln is the United States' first degree-granting historically black university. Joe went there on a minority student scholarship. Langston Hughes is another poet who attended this institution although, unlike Joe, he did NOT rack up over $150 in library fines.

Joe graduated just in time to be drafted. Somewhat reluctant to go off to Vietnam, Joe enlisted for another year and was sent to Monterey, California, to learn Russian at the Defense Language Institute. He did learn Russian and was then sent to Fort Huachuca, Arizona, to be a POW interrogator because he refused to sign up for another year. After graduating from there he was chosen to role-play as a Russian POW for Green Berets to interrogate. He was then sent to Fort Hood, Texas, to the 529th MI company (see his Army poems) where he taught English to brides of returning soldiers and was chosen to curate the Army's collection of Bibles in foreign languages, including one in Hawaiian that mysteriously disappeared. He got out of the Army and went to California to begin his new adventure and ended up briefly selling vacuum cleaners door to door. He re-enlisted and went back to Fort Huachuca where, somehow, he ended up writing Army manuals. His first publication was not the epic poem about epic stuff he was thinking of writing but was "Nuclear, Biological and Chemical Warfare" in which soldiers were told—no matter what horror unfolded to—"continue the mission."

Joe left the Army after seven years and got a job as a technical writer in Waco (Jerusalem by the Brazos) and then Dallas. Then he got a job at Control Data, Inc. where he helped design and write the first computer-based training ever. He also obtained access to Control Data's "Plato" network of mainframe computers at universities and corporations and at once created a Poetry Newsgroup for persons to post poems, talk about poetry and for him to collaborate with Tim Smith (who lived in Carmel, California and had access to the network) on creating fake comic poets, comic poems and more. Connie, the love of his life, also had access to the system and was amused and saw through it all, so pretty soon Joe moved to Minnesota to be with her. Joe's daughter from a previous marriage also moved up there. Joe flew out to California where he and Tim met, created the "Parapark Tapes," together and began a collaboration and friendship which resulted in (among much else) the "Limerick Homer." Joe married Connie in 1990 and their daughter Johanna was born!

In Minnesota Joe got a job at Cray Research writing the user's manual for the Cray YMP Supercomputer. Through this job, Joe got access to the USENET: a precursor to the internet and at once spent much of his time contributing to the books and poetry newsgroups. It was here that he met the Great Russian who would eventually publish him in the poetry annual, *Fulcrum*. Joe also founded the "O'Tooles," This was a blissome group of blissome persons writing blissome this and thats. Joe wrote a story about meeting one of them called "Well Met in Minnesota," which was a big hit ... so much so that there was an article, "Bards of the Internet," about it in *Time Magazine*. Joe was invited to be a featured speaker at the Third annual Conference on Computers, Freedom and Privacy in San Francisco in 1994 where he extemporized poems about J. Edgar Hoover to an audience of geeks and FBI agents, was told by the head of the Homicide Unit in NYC that he loved his performance, and where he was given a sequence of Star Trek sonnets that were quite good by a lady whose name he wishes he could remember.

Joe then was accepted into the English PhD program at the University of Minnesota. He thought he would be a professor. Ha! He loved it there though and loved his teachers: Chester Anderson, the editor of "Portrait of the Artist as a Young Man," a great Joyce scholar; Tom Clayton, a very great Shakespearean scholar who would oversee the dissertation Joe would never complete; and the guy who was hired in the Sixties, somehow got tenure after publishing a paper on Keats, then, happily, never published anything else. Joe also met Stuart Reike there, who was a student in a class he taught and is a damn fine poet and musician who composed a song about Joe and the devil and, maybe, Robert Johnson.

Joe returned to work as a technical writer after passing his oral exams and insisting (and carrying it off) that there were hidden depths in *Titus Andronicus*. Joe had to study *The Faerie Queene* in depth to pass the exam and sometimes still shows symptoms.

Then, in 2002, after renewing contacts with the editors of *Fulcrum*, he began to be published. His poems appear in every issue of *Fulcrum* and in one issue of *Rattapallax* No. 12 (as detailed in the Acknowledgements to this book). He also had three books published by Owl Oak Press: *The Diamond at the End of Time* (Owl Oak Press, 2006), *The Dark Bark: Poetry and Songs of Rin Tin Tin* (Owl Oak Press, 2006), The Limerick Homer (Owl Oak Press, 2008).

In August 2012 he began to write his novel *The Chains of the Sea* (search for it on Amazon! Please!) and finished all 752 pages by November 6, 2012. The novel recounts the quest of "The Visionary Company" to find "The Diamond at the End of Time" and reach God who has not been paying attention. One review says: "Oh my, step aside Samael for Joe Green shall ride on through. With a psychedelic mix of literature culture, music, pop art and motor drama weirdness Joe Green creates a dynamic and engaging fantasy world full of Eliot's cats, dead poets, ray guns and a whole heap besides. There are no illegal substances required with this book as the lines themselves will hypnotize you, spellbind and daze you into an alter-reality, another dimension, well, several all at once with eyes focused on a ragged troupe of disparate travelers through time and space, immortal one feels as they discuss the lengthy and tangled web in which they exist, Godot with a large cast awaiting the final outcome, a mystery to all."

Since then Joe has written some other poems that will appear in the newest edition of *Fulcrum* in 2015. Joe hopes he can get his mojo back.

Joe would also like to mention that he saw W. H. Auden read at Marquette in 1966 to a small group in the student union, and Joe still hasn't gotten over his luck, and that he also saw Allen Ginsberg read at the University of Wisconsin–Milwaukee after students marched there with the Ginz because he was denied a chance to read at Marquette because he was a homosexual—unlike, one supposes, Mr. Auden. A strange world! Also please read Joe's poem about Joe's beloved Uncle Joe meeting Auden.

www.ingramcontent.com/pod-product-compliance
Lightning Source LLC
Chambersburg PA
CBHW031600110426
42742CB00036B/259